LEADERSHIP FORMULA

THE SECRET WITHIN THE SYSTEM
BASED ON ONE SIMPLE PRINCIPLE

JUSTIN ATEN

Copyright © 2018 by Justin Aten.

All rights reserved. No part of this publication may be reproduced, distributed or transmitted in any form or by any means, including photocopying, recording, or other electronic or mechanical methods, without the prior written permission of the publisher, except in the case of brief quotations embodied in critical reviews and certain other noncommercial uses permitted by copyright law. For permission requests, write to the publisher, addressed "Attention: Permissions Coordinator," at the address below.

SamuelHannah Creative Designs, LLC
116 Honeysuckle Way
Flower Mound, TX 75028
TheLeadershipFormulaBook.com

Editing by Katie Chambers, Beacon Point
Illustrations by Samuel Aten
Cover design: facebook.com/topbookdesigner

Ordering Information:
Quantity sales. Special discounts are available on quantity purchases by corporations, associations, and others. Contact the "Special Sales Department" at the address above.

The Leadership Formula/ Justin Aten. 1st ed.
ISBN 978-1-7913918-2-9
FREE templates: TheLeadershipFormulaBook.com

Contents

INTRODUCTION 1

Part 1: THE FOUNDATION 12

1. THE SECRET WITHIN THE SYSTEM 13

2. CORE PRINCIPLES 23

3. PROBLEM SOLVING 35

PART 2: PARTS OF THE SYSTEM 44

4. THE DAILY HUDDLE 45

5. THE WEEKLY GAME PLAN 75

6. MONTHLY IMPROVEMENT EVENTS 87

7. SUMMARY OF THE SYSTEM 107

PART 3: TIPS FOR SUCCESS 114

8. PITFALLS TO AVOID 115

9. LEADERSHIP QUALITIES 123

10. REMEMBER THIS 135

11. LOOKING FORWARD 139

*Dedicated to my wife and our 2.5 kids,
Samuel, Hannah and Maggie the Goldendoodle*

And to my parents. With a special thanks to my stepmother, Harriet, for her ardent belief...

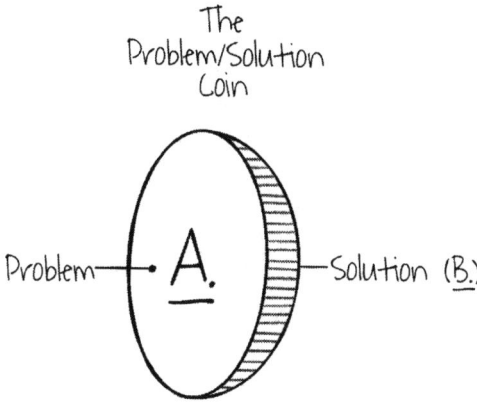

"The flip side of any problem is a solution waiting to be created."

INTRODUCTION

Sleeping in the doctor's basement with a cougar and a monkey nearby was not part of the plan.

A few days prior, the administrator of the medical clinic in a small town had gone missing. No clues, no messages, no note—just gone.

The clinic was an active place, a pillar of life in a town of around nine thousand that ballooned to over thirty thousand one week every year during the national mud racing championships.

One of the founding doctors of the clinic—an icon in the community and a kind, older family man who was also the proud owner of a monkey and a pet cougar, had provided a place for me to stay while I filled in as the interim administrator.

As the search for the missing administrator continued and the weeks wore on, I made myself useful, taking care of things as needed, helping out with the staff and getting to know the community.

Radio campaigns with jingles at the end were completed, bills were paid, and two additional doctors were hired. The founding doctors were pleased with the progress, and when they determined the former administrator would not return, the doctors asked me to stay on as the administrator full-time.

This was my first real experience with leadership. And as well as it started, it didn't last long.

I made the mistake of discussing payment responsibilities with a patient in a public area. Some of the staff raised concerns regarding plans to expand the clinic—possibly those whose new offices may have ended up in an area with fewer windows and less sunshine.

Then a colleague turned from collaborator to saboteur and convinced the doctors that she could do the job better.

After three short but intense months, I was asked to leave. It happens. I had no regrets and was left with mostly good memories but also a lingering question:

"What is good leadership and how do you do it?"

Leadership

It is well known that bad leadership can have a horrible impact: poor morale, low engagement, high stress, high turn-over rate, lack of growth, lost revenue, lack of fulfillment, boredom, health problems, job changes, business failure, and strife at work and at home.

Good leadership, on the other hand, can produce a high-performing team, high levels of engagement, job satisfaction, competitiveness, higher earnings, increased company value, joy, stability, balance, respect, peace at home and the ability to help others.

In order to achieve those results, you need to be an effective leader. But what really makes a leader effective?

Most people who find themselves in leadership positions do not have adequate training and frequently end up making it up as they go. Although some do find a way to get by, they are frequently left with the sense that there must be a better way. There must be a way to lead well.

What really makes a leader effective?

Occasionally, the lessons learned from bad bosses (what not to do) and good bosses might be enough to get started as a leader but generally will only take you so far. Even the great leadership principles found in books and the excellent anecdotal stories of leadership fall short in fully equipping a new leader when the demands and challenges of leading a team are high.

A few years after my initial plunge into leadership, I found myself starting over in a venture that would lead to more leadership learning.

I moved with my wife from Chicago to Texas, so she could complete her medical training. It was right after the dot-com bust of 2002 and not the best time to find a job in the investment business.

After several months with no success, I found temporary work on a data project for a healthcare company. When the project was done, I was hired on full time as an analyst, which eventually led to other roles and increasing levels of responsibility within the company. Eight years, four positions, and two acquisitions later I was asked to lead a data and analytics team of about twenty-five people in three cities.

Up to that point, things had gone fairly well. My responsibilities had included leading projects where the cross-functional teams were disbanded when the work was done. In the meantime, I had completed an MBA, read plenty of leadership books, and made the study of leadership a priority.

Despite what I thought I knew after many years in the workplace as well as a good amount of training, I found myself again in a situation where my leadership skills left me in a corner with no easy way out.

As the company I was employed by worked through the integration of various systems, processes, and people due to the latest acquisition, one of the key leaders on my team took another role within the company leaving a large gap in our team's ability to perform. When he left, I discovered previously unknown problems, poor processes and a slightly dysfunctional team. All of which had been masked by his deep expertise and herculean efforts.

At the same time the demands of our internal clients (the sales and client management team) had skyrocketed as they sought to aggressively serve the needs of our combined customer and potential customer base.

Between the various tools of both companies, the different processes that had not yet been synchronized, the changes in personnel, and the high demands of our clients, our system broke.

Our clients were consistently complaining that the results were not good enough; team members were fighting; and many of us were working extremely hard just to keep up. I remember being up late at night (as I was on most nights) working on last minute deadlines while our family was on "vacation" in Costa Rica. I was burned out.

Fortunately, right at that moment Coach K showed up. He started working with me to implement a system for team leadership and performance. And slowly I could start to see the light at the end of the tunnel.

You Need A System

The system taught by Coach K was built on the fundamentals of team leadership as pioneered and practiced by one of the most successful and innovative companies in the world. Using it enabled my team to not only survive but thrive.

Having started as an automated loom manufacturer, Toyota may have adopted these principles partially out of necessity. After WWII, with little money to invest in other catalysts for growth, Toyota focused on making the most of what they did have—people and some important ideas about "systems" from W. Edwards Deming, an American from Sioux City, Iowa.

Ultimately, the people, process, and principle-based system for continuous improvement they developed tapped into human potential, systems thinking and the maximization of collaborative team efforts via what is now commonly referred to as "Lean" or "Lean Thinking." Frequently misunderstood (in part due to the name), this system focuses on structured problem solving, guided collaboration and a deep respect for the capability of people to improve the work they do.

Using this system helped my team to increase our productivity by 57 percent in less than one year. Our turnaround time to deliver quality products was reduced by over 33 percent. More importantly, our team members were engaged, and our customers were happy!

In addition to the business success we achieved after utilizing the system for a short time, I was surprised and very pleased to witness the profound impact on our team members. For example:

- One formerly painfully shy analyst presented to the CEO as if she were the President of Toastmasters.
- A tech-savvy introvert (affectionately known as "Oz"), who had long been only a sole-contributor, successfully developed and led a team of other "wizards".
- A skilled mid-level analyst, who previously had three managers check his work before a senior company official presented it to the client, completed the work independently and presented directly to the client with even better results.
- A respected team leader, who was frequently frustrated by sales executives, learned to manage relationships effectively and over-deliver at the same time.
- A highly capable director, who had plateaued in her career, earned respect and moved forward, eventually holding several vice president roles.

All of these individuals were able to break through to the next level of their capabilities and careers because they were part of a system for team performance that also developed the potential within people.

Personally, in addition to reducing the stress and headaches, I found joy again in work, and in the span of three years, due to increased responsibilities, I was able to double my income.

After many previous attempts to improve my leadership skills by varying methods, including study, "leadership training" and working harder, I realized that the system was the secret.

A good leadership system will help you maximize your team results and leadership success whether you are a solopreneur, part of a start-up company, or leading a team in a large, established organization.

Maybe you are good enough, smart enough, and doggone it people like you, so you will do fine without a system. But if you want to be really good, see incredible results, find fulfillment and consistently grow other leaders, you need a system. Maximizing your success means more than just getting by.

The system is the secret.

I would have been happy if using the system had simply helped our team to get out of the hole we were in and do better work, but it accomplished so much more. Here are some of the benefits we saw in less than one year:

- Increased productivity
- Improved engagement
- Engaged remote team members
- Improved product quality
- Reduced turn-around time

- Reduced costs
- Increased revenue
- Increased personal financial growth
- Reduced stress
- Improved job satisfaction
- Increased professional skills growth
- Increased innovation

Since that initial experience, I have used this system with all types of teams: business intelligence, product development, sales and client management, legal, supply chain, procurement, staffing, technical support, etc. It works, and it makes life so much better for leaders, for the team and for customers.

Imagine the joy of a legal team that reduces its turnaround time so much that people can no longer say, "It's stuck in legal!" Or a procurement team that avoids "plane crash" type events such as ordering the wrong size heart valve for a surgery? Or a manager who finds a way to engage team members in the process of improving results without feeling like she is losing control?

Beyond principles of leadership or anecdotal stories about leadership situations, this is a system for leadership. Don't get me wrong; I love leadership principles and there are many great stories about leadership. And yes, they can be very helpful. But sometimes we need a clear and practical roadmap that shows where we are going and the turn-by-turn instructions of how to get there.

And of course, some of us are just cookbook people. We need to read the recipe so that we can follow the steps and make something that looks just like the nice glossy photo in the book. Enviable principles and entertaining stories that are intriguing but difficult to apply to daily work life just don't cut the mustard when you are struggling to keep your head above water.

I remember reading about and being excited about the concept of servant-leadership. But when it came time to actually lead and serve both customers and my team, figuring out how to apply the concept in daily work-life was a different matter. This system is how.

I have attempted to keep things simple while retaining the essentials and making the concepts accessible to anyone who is responding to the call to leadership and recognizes the need for a better way.

Leadership is a journey...it is always better to have a map.

Whether you are the CEO of a new technology start-up, a recently promoted manager in a large company, or a proud new parent of triplets, you lead teams. It can be tempting to forge ahead and just "get by" with what you already know. But leadership is a journey. And as with any journey, it is always better to have a map.

So, read on. Absorb the details and secrets of the system. Incorporate them with your team and watch your people and your revenue grow. The concepts are simple but will require some work. Just take it step by step.

I wish you the very best on your leadership journey. I hope that this helps you to enjoy it more.

Part 1: THE FOUNDATION

Chapter 1

1. THE SECRET WITHIN THE SYSTEM

"You will never be the Dragon Warrior until you have learned the secret of the Dragon Scroll."

- *Master Shifu, Kung Fu Panda*

When you step into the role of leader / manager / coach, you take on an extremely important role indeed. Beyond "doing a good job" and making sure that business is getting done, you take on the role of leading and growing people—and by doing so, you have the potential to make a massive difference.

If there were a magical pill with a secret ingredient that would transform you into a better leader, would you take it? Or if there was an ancient "Dragon Scroll" with the one and only hidden secret to great leadership, would you want to open the scroll to find out what it is? What if the real secret to great leadership were almost that easy: a mindset and framework for thinking that if applied properly would make a radical impact on your team, your company, and your life?

It's easy to find stories that provide a glimpse of what leadership looks like in certain situations. Some of our family's most beloved movies involve an unlikely hero who rises to the occasion and takes a leadership role when danger threatens. But how do you translate inspiring stories into your own real-life leadership experience? Are you going to show up for work dressed like Po in Kung Fu Panda?

There are so many perspectives and opinions on what is really required for good leadership. How can you be sure that you are doing it right?

"...to go before or show the way..."

According to the Word Reference app by Random House, Leadership is... "the position or function of being a leader, one that leads." And to lead is... "to go before or show the way; to conduct by guiding; to influence." That's not bad in terms of a definition but when it comes to practice, knowing how to lead well can be a little less clear.

Is it your character or personality that makes you a good or successful leader? Is it the knowledge you gain through your training, education, experience, and mentorship? Or is it your drive, determination, will, ambition and high standards that makes the difference? Can you sum it up as "influence"? If you listen to many Hollywood movies, you will just need, "...the will to do what is necessary." Or, maybe there is some deeper, mystical understanding that can only be gained by embarking on a long and perilous journey?

We do know that poor leadership can lead to failure for the leader and those they lead. At any level it can be devastating, whether leading a country, a company, a charity, a start-up, or a family.

Good leadership, on the other hand, can provide a path to many good things: personal success, business growth, positive social impact, family stability, and economic abundance.

Personally, I have led successfully, and I have failed at leading. I have learned and had the benefit of great mentors. Each one provided meaningful lessons that I now incorporate into the context of a leadership system.

"Sometimes you just have to make do."

There was Doyle, for example, the owner of a gas station where I worked during college, pumping gas for customers the old-fashioned way. Doyle would say, "Sometimes you just have to make do." A lesson learned from life on the farm and applied when an underground gas pipe breaks at two in the morning and there is no one to fix it but you. Even if the temperature is many degrees below zero, you just "make do."

Then there was Larry, the owner of the antique store and picture frame shop, who would always say, "We don't make changes—we make adjustments." Having to make a "change" to a frame sounded like we had done something wrong. Making an "adjustment", on the other hand, sounded like we were doing even more to please the customer's wishes. It became a positive thing.

I have served under good and bad leaders; worked hard, struggled, stressed, and celebrated success as a teacher, a coach, a front-line employee, a manager, a director, a vice president, a start-up founder, an inventor, a writer and a father.

What I've found is that knowledge, character, personality and even attitude by themselves are not enough to lead well. Of course, each one is important. But if you have the right mindset for leadership and a system, you will be much more successful and will be more likely to reach your goals, be fulfilled, and thrive.

Read any business magazine, *Forbes*, *Fortune*, *Fast Company*, *Inc.*, etc., and you will hear stories of people and companies succeeding through trials and tribulations by tapping into an overcoming mindset, sticking it out, and by some degree of "luck" or chance. I lived on those stories for a while. They are inspiring in a way. They can be intoxicating too. But like most drugs, the effect wears off and you find yourself the same as before *unless* you are able to glean some inspiration or nugget of wisdom that you can actually apply to your circumstances.

> ...*knowledge, character, personality and even attitude by themselves are not enough to lead well.*

Unfortunately, inspiration comes and goes and wisdom for one circumstance may not apply to another situation. But a mindset that applies to all levels of leadership situations and a system that provides the structure and tools needed for any team to be successful is powerful.

Ultimately, leadership must be about going somewhere. And if you are going somewhere, you must have a clear picture of where you want to end up. Fuzzy, moving targets are hard to hit. But before you head off in the direction of your clearly defined goals, it is also important to know where you currently are. Can you imagine using a GPS system's directions to get to Chicago if the GPS thinks you are in Wichita and you are in Dallas? Talk about some bad directions!

Let's talk about the leadership mindset that can be used to take you and your team wherever it is that you want to go. This is the "Dragon Scroll" secret of leadership.

The Leadership Formula

The simple formula for the "secret within the system" team leader mindset is: $B=A-C^2$. (B equals A minus C squared). For a simple memory device, think of the 1985 movie, "Back to the Future" (Bac 2 the Future). '*B*' stands for where you want to go; your destination, goal, or vision of where you want to <u>B</u>e; '*A*' stands for where you currently <u>A</u>re now or today; C^2 are the challenges you face, and more importantly, the root <u>C</u>auses of those challenges. You remove the challenges by addressing the root <u>C</u>auses with

Countermeasures so that you can get where you want to go.

This formula may seem very simple—and it should because it is. But don't be fooled by its simplicity. Most profound things are actually simple.

> *"Making the simple complicated is commonplace; making the complicated simple...that's creativity."*
> *- Charles Mingus*

There is a lot of wisdom in this formula when you use it to organize your thinking and clarify each of the variables in your situation: be clear about where you want to go; be clear about where you are today; be clear about the root causes of the things that are holding you back; and be very clear about the countermeasures you will put in place to address the root causes so that you can move forward and reach your desired destination.

Let's be honest—most of us start a part of this process—we get clear about where we want to be, and we even start to recognize some of the things that are holding us back. But we stop there. We don't see an immediate solution so instead of digging deeper to the root cause, we mentally give up and then start to complain, "Yes, I'd like to have that reach my dreams, but I can't because x, y and z." Make sure you tune in to these voices and challenge them—they are false but if you are not careful, you may not even realize that you've started believing un-true assumptions that masquerade as reasonable excuses.

Dig deeper. Find the root cause and address it. Move forward towards your goals, dreams and ideals. You will see the components of this thinking process played out over and over in different areas as we get into the details of the system for team leadership.

Dig deeper. Find the root cause...

The formula is both the foundational mindset for leadership and a tool that you can use to analyze a situation and come up with a plan.

Fig. 1: TLF Arrow

Using this tool is simple. First, get very clear about where you want to be and where you are. Next, identify the root causes of the challenges that are keeping you from getting to where you want to be. Then determine the countermeasures that you will employ to overcome the things that are holding you back so that you can reach your goals.

This is a mindset and a process that you will need to apply over and over. As new challenges arise, you will need to remind yourself where it is that you want to be, so you don't get sidetracked or make decisions that take you in a different direction. Then when goals are met, new goals will need to be developed and the process starts over.

Here's the funny thing about the leadership formula...

The Formula Can Be Seen as a Pattern Within the System – Just Like Fractals

If you are not yet familiar with fractals, think of seashells, cauliflower, ferns or human lungs—at varying levels of magnification—the same structures and patterns are seen.

As noted in Wired magazine, "Earth's Most Stunning Natural Fractal Patterns—The mathematical beauty of fractals is that infinite complexity is formed with relatively simple equations. By iterating or repeating fractal-generating equations many times, random outputs create beautiful patterns that are unique, yet recognizable."

The leadership formula is similar to fractals in that you can see the same pattern repeating itself at varying levels of the system. To test the formula, look to see if it holds up—think through whether you could apply it to varying types of leadership situations. Does it work for buying an ice-cream cone with the kids as well as leading a country? If it works, it should pass this strange but simple type of test.

Just like the fractal patterns we can see in nature, the leadership formula should work no matter how small or large the leadership situation we focus in on.

A similar concept is the Fibonacci spiral—a shell-like spiral that is created by connecting the corners of triangles that follow the Fibonacci sequence of numbers identified by Leonardo Pisano Bogollo (1170 - 1250).

Fig. 2: the Fibonacci spiral

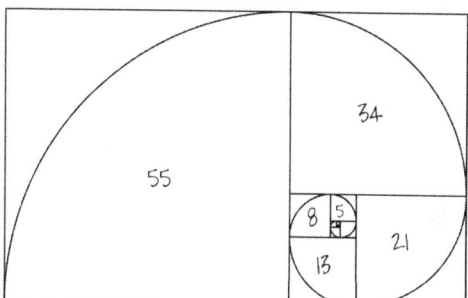

"Similar to fractals, the Fibonacci sequence recognizes patterns in what might otherwise appear to be chaotic and random."

Just as fractal patterns and the Fibonacci sequence make sense out of what otherwise might appear to be chaos, the leadership formula does the same for leadership situations. Whether you focus intensely on solving a problem or adjust the magnification back a little to the structure for people collaboration, the leadership formula applies.

The Leadership Formula: $B=A-C^2$

> B = where you want to be
> A = where you are now
> C^2 = the root causes for not being there and the countermeasure actions to correct

Considering all of the components or aspects of leadership that you need to have a handle on in order to lead well, you need a pattern to subdue the chaos, a formula that allows you to make sense of it and bring order to it. The leadership formula helps you to do so.

CHAPTER 2

2. CORE PRINCIPLES

Just as having a car without gas will get you nowhere, a system without principles won't do you much good. Once you have a car, you need a little gas to make it go. Here are the guidelines—the principles that make this system work. They are the "gas" for your vehicle.

Respect

Leadership is about leading people to a new place. Whether it is a new hire, a potential investor, or an upset customer, you must have your mind in the right place so that you can lead people forward to where you want to be with skill and confidence.

For this, you need the foundational people-mindset principle: Always start with respect. As an individual contributor or front-line worker (I started out sorting cans in the back of a grocery store), your primary focus was getting the work done that needed to be done. As a leader, your primary focus is people. Obviously, you are still concerned that quality work is being done but now almost all of the work you do will be through other people; therefore, you must have the right mindset. In everything that you do, start with an attitude of respect. If you hold this attitude in your mind for every new situation, you will go a long way.

This means respect for people, respect for their time, respect for their opinions, respect, respect, respect. In every situation, approach the situation and the people associated with it with an attitude of respect. This principle applies no matter what is going on and especially when there is a problem.

Imagine that you have discovered a problem or a situation happening with one of your team members. If you approach their desk with the mindset this person has made a mistake or caused a problem, it will be immediately apparent to the team member, and they will likely become defensive. If, however, you approach the team member with respect, they will sense this as well.

Don't assume that the person has made a mistake. Instead, you assume that there was a problem in the *process*. Rather than having an antagonistic interaction, you will be able to have an open and collaborative discussion. When the team member feels supported and respected (instead of judged and criticized), they will be free to think creatively, to engage deeper, and to take responsibility for resolving the problem.

Respect is the emotional currency for people in the digital age. It is something that we can pay to people, and it immediately pays back! Respect for people; respect for their efforts and accomplishments; respect for their time; and respect for their potential.

In some cases, you may have a team member who is not performing well. You may not know why. Maybe they were previously a star performer, and something happened. Or they are new to the team and now you are worried that you made the wrong choice. If you have respect for their potential, then you allow your mind to get creative and to find a way to bring out the best in them.

Maybe you need a new approach to training that is tailored to the person's learning style. Maybe you need to have a discussion with them and give them the time and freedom to resolve a personal issue that is holding them back from performing well at work.

If you've ever seen the Sandra Bullock movie *The Blind Side,* you know how valuable this can be. In the movie, Michael Oher is a football player with great potential. But he is getting pushed around on the field and not contributing to the team. Then something happens—his coach defends him, and he realizes that he is part of a team and essentially part of the football team family.

Having a strong bent toward "protection," he decides it is time to defend his "family" which includes the quarterback. On the next play, he pushes his opponent so far back that he throws him over the fence and out of the field. The rest (as they say) is history. He goes on to be an NFL player.

It never would have happened if someone hadn't had enough respect for him as a person to take the time to understand and work with him.

Clarity

Ask yourself this clarifying question before any important meeting or dealing with any situation: What do you want to get out of it? This was Coach K's favorite question to ask and it is a good one. By starting with a respectful attitude and clarifying your goals (desired end results), you are much more likely to be successful. You are respectfully considerate of the other person and you know what you are aiming for, so you are much more likely to end up with a good result.

I've read business books that will go so far as to say that providing clarity is THE #1 core job of any leader. Clarify your goals and then clarify expectations for the team so that they know what the end result should look like. This will keep you all on the same page and moving in the right direction.

Value

This may seem obvious, but you must let your customer decide what is valuable and what they are, therefore, willing to pay for. It is easy for any company or team to become complacent and out of date with what their customer sees as valuable *today* and start trying to make decisions without getting the critical input needed directly from the customer.

This means that you, as a leader, must frequently interact with and receive feedback from customers to make sure you are up to date on their current needs and their perspectives on your products and services. If their needs or definition of value changes and you are not aware of it, they will be forced to go somewhere else.

As a leader, as you gain new insights about your customer or where the market is headed, make sure you update your team.

In the past, some leaders would withhold these insights in an attempt to retain power with an, "I know more than you do" attitude. In today's world of social media, your team members may gain insights into customer trends that even you don't have. You need to have a "sharing economy" approach to sharing information or your competition will move faster than you to meet your customers' needs.

Flow

Once you understand what value is to your customer, focus on making it flow. This means that your entire process should flow without interruption from the beginning to the end—all the way to the customer. Within your process, things should happen at the appropriate speed without unnecessary waiting or extra steps, so the customer receives value at the timing and pace they need it. Look for this flow. Learn to see it—or see when it is not happening. This is sometimes referred to "eyes for flow".

Waste

As you look at the process of providing value to the customer, you will likely identify things that are not bringing value to the customer and should be stopped as well as roadblocks, pot holes, or speedbumps in the process that need to be removed or fixed. These can be considered as waste—things that use up your resources and do not bring value to the customer.

There is a saying related to this: "Eliminate waste, not people." Sometimes companies that are only focused on the bottom line and quick solutions decide that the quickest way to improve margins is to eliminate people. Instead, if you eliminate the unnecessary waste from the process, the things that the customer does not value, you will need to keep your good people because customers will be satisfied, and you will either gain new customers or be able to add new products and services.

The Place of Work

Mistakes and broken processes are not necessarily a crime, but they may in fact be stealing time and attention from employees that is not necessary. Like a good detective, when evaluating work processes and improvement opportunities, you must go and see where the work actually happens every day.

Looking at charts and data will give you clues but not a full understanding of how work gets done. Don't try to manage, fix or lead without understanding how things really happen. There is only one place to really do that—the place where the work is done. Without the full picture of the situation and input from the people who actually do the front-line work, as a leader you will be steering partially blind.

If you have ever watched or read Sherlock Holmes stories, you've probably noticed that he has very astute powers of observation. His conversations go something like this, "I noticed that your right pant leg has mud on it and therefore your butler must be on vacation visiting his uncle in the West Indies..." Little clues allow sharp detectives to reconstruct events and gain a more complete understanding of what is really happening.

So, go and see. Go to the scene of work. It's a crime not to. When you get there, take your time to observe and be curious about all of the details. Just remember that you are not there to accuse any criminals—make sure that you start with respect! And keep your focus on the process.

Process Focus

I mentioned that when you have an issue with a team member, but you focus on the process, team members won't feel guilty, afraid, or worried about being reprimanded when mistakes occur. They recognize that the focus is on the process. Did the process not work for some reason? Or did we not follow the process? If you followed the process and an error still occurred, then you know that you need to fix the process, not the people.

Coach K used to say, "Manage the process, not the people." Most people assume when they step into a position of leadership that they need to manage people. But if you focus on managing the process through your people, your team can engage collaboratively to fix the process and make it better, which will lead to better performance. Instead of focusing on managing people, you can focus on training and supporting people as *they* improve the process.

Resolve

Resolve happens at the beginning of any leadership opportunity when you resolve to do it and to do it well; not that you will do everything perfectly all the time, but you're resolved to constantly improve and work toward perfection. The old adage "It's hard to steer a parked car" is true for leadership.

It is good to learn and prepare, but at some point, you just have to resolve to start doing it and resign yourself that you are never going to be as prepared as you would like to be. You know enough to get started. You will learn more along the way.

Resolve also happens along the leadership journey when things get tough and when it seems like there is no way out of a difficult situation. When a situation seems hopeless, you must resolve to continue. You must resolve to not give up. You must resolve to have hope, no matter what.

One of my favorite leadership stories came out of the 2006 NBA championships. My family and I have become Mavericks fans, so I was pumped when the Mavericks won the first two games of the NBA championship series. Things were looking very good for the Mavs and you could sense the excitement.

Then I heard a news report about Dwyane Wade, one of the star players for the opposing Miami Heat. After suffering the second loss, he was very down and called a good friend. He told his friend about his woes and how he felt. He had basically thrown in the towel. His friend said one thing that I believe changed the entire outcome of that series.

After listening to all of Wade's woes, he said (something like), "Wait a minute—that was *supposed* to happen?" Wait—what? Losing the first two games of the NBA championship series—the thing that was getting him down and causing him to lose self-confidence and throw in the towel on his hopes and dreams of winning a championship, was supposed to happen?! Yes...

The impact on Dwyane Wade's mindset cannot be understated. If what he thought was failure was supposed to happen, then there was still hope that his dream of winning was possible. This simple shift in the way he was thinking about past events allowed a spark of hope back into Wade's mindset. And with that hope came resolve.

This is pure speculation on my part but I'm guessing his thoughts were something like this: "Sure, we lost two games in a row. But I can still do everything I can, and along with my team, surely, we can at least win the next game on our home court. We've done it before. Why not? We can do it again."

With a clean mental slate, he could focus on winning one game at a time, which is a lot easier than trying to mentally deal with loss and imagine winning the entire series. The Heat did win the next game—and the next game and, as Mavericks fans can painfully remember (as we slowly watched our seemingly iron-clad championship fade away) the championship.

Hope

If you haven't experienced it yet, at some point in your managerial and leadership career, you will experience challenges and setbacks. Some of them might even seem disastrous. Look at the story of what Thomas Edison did when his entire lab and factory burned completely to the ground:

The next morning, one of his team found him and asked desperately, "What shall we do?" His answer? Without hesitating, he said, "Rebuild."

You must resolve to have a mindset of hope, no matter how dire or difficult the circumstances become.

It was always funny to me that the *Star Wars* movies seemed to place such a high premium on hope. The first movie to hit the theaters in 1978 was subtitled *A New Hope*. The most recent movie to hit theaters (forty years later), *The Last Jedi*, placed a high premium on hope. Then one day, I began to understand the reason. When people lose hope, they throw in the towel. They give up. They relinquish their will to continue doing whatever it is they were doing: living—competing—striving for some accomplishment at work.

As a leader you must know this. If strong winds come against your team and they are barraged with bad news and it seems like there is no hope for success, they will give up to some degree. Your job as a leader is to keep hope alive. No matter how late in the game or how many points your team is down, you must continue to redefine hope, so your people can believe and continue moving forward. They must not lose hope in the cause or in themselves.

Hope is not something you bring to the forefront of your team's attention every day. It is something you will need to focus on when the time is right, when the chips are down, when you have suffered a setback of some sort. It is an ingredient of leadership that you will need to have ready when needed.

Growth and Innovation

Create a respect-filled environment. Keep the desired end result in mind. Let your customer define what value is. Keep that value flowing to the customer. Eliminate the waste in the process. Go to the place where the work is done to understand what really happens. Help your team to improve the process. Resolve to get started, keep going and keep hope alive for your team.

As you incorporate these leadership behaviors into your implementation of this system for leading teams, your business will begin to get under control and you will be positioned to grow and innovate. This is when business starts to get fun. Next, we'll talk about how.

Chapter 3:

3. PROBLEM SOLVING

"Sir, I can fix those glasses!"

- Navin R. Johnson (Steve Martin) in The Jerk.

Now that you have the leadership formula and you know the key principles needed for success with the system, let's look at how the team leadership formula can be applied to problem solving—this is the last foundational element and the beginning of the system.

When leading teams there are five primary areas to think about as you deliver value to your customer: principles, people, processes, pit-falls, and problems.

And one thing is absolutely true for every problem you will face: the flip side of that problem is the opportunity to create a solution. As undesirable as a problem may initially seem, it is helpful to realize that if viewed properly, there is a related opportunity to make things better. Knowing this as a leader changes the way we view problems. Whereas normal thinking would tell you that it is best to avoid problems, once you have the "problem-->solution" mindset, it becomes easy to recognize problems for what they truly are, an opportunity in disguise.

Isn't this just some mental trick that tries to make something good out of something bad? No, this is the truth. Just look at all of the good things that have been invented—they were all the result of someone solving a problem or providing something that was missing.

Name anything in this world created by people and you will find behind the thing a problem that created the need for the solution we now enjoy. This mindset of acknowledging, accepting, and even appreciating problems will set you up for success in whatever you do.

How do you currently feel about problems? Most people can identify a problem, but they stop there and don't do anything about it because the problem appears to be beyond their control. For many of us, we can deal with little problems that are within our comfort level. When something seems bigger than our confidence and comfort level, it is likely to cause a negative reaction such as fear, frustration, or anger. Those reactions generally stifle the creative thinking needed to come up with solutions.

How do you currently feel about problems?

In addition to the right mindset toward problems, it is important to understand how to increase your creative capacity and problem-solving skills. The easiest way to do this is by sharing the problem and involving a team. Yes, a key part of leadership is dealing with and solving problems but NOT in a vacuum all by yourself. A leader who tries to be the "oracle" or grand-master problem solver will be less effective than one who recognizes the value of having a team that is empowered to solve problems and has the tools and skills to do so.

The A3 Problem-Solving Method

Empowering your team to solve problems means you will need to give them some tools to succeed and the right to fail. When people are fearful of the consequences of failing, they don't take risks and risks are necessary to solve problems. In order to be consistently effective, your team will need to be trained in the use of a structured problem-solving tool.

> *Having a structure doesn't take away from the creative side of problem solving, it just guides you through the process.*

The A3 problem-solving method got its name from the European size of paper that was originally used but you can use the size paper that is most readily available. 8 ½ by 11-inch paper works just fine. It is simply a one-page document broken into sections that walks you through the problem-solution process. The magic comes from the structure that it provides to the creative thinking process. After going through the simple process, you will have a solid understanding of the problem, an outline of the current state, a proposed solution, and the sketch of a pathway to get there.

To get started, divide a horizontal paper into three equal sections by drawing two vertical lines. Now draw three horizontal lines so that you have nine sections. In some cases (like the example) you may want to use more than one box to fill in the details for a particular section.

Fig. 3: Problem-Solving A3

Problem	Improved State	Solution Proposed
What is it?	What does success look like?	Physical Process People
Current State		Action Plan
How is it working/not working?		Who. What. When.
Root Cause		Measures
5 Whys Fishbone		Now=_ End=_ Risks=_ How will you continue to improve?

You can use a pre-made template or print your own version for this, but I want you to see how easy this is just starting with a blank sheet of paper.

Download FREE templates at:

TheLeadershipFormulaBook.com

Starting in the top left box and going down and then to the right, fill in the topic for each section:

P = Problem
C = Current State
R = Root Cause
I = Ideal State
S = Solution
A = Action Plan
M = Measures
(use extras boxes as needed for a particular section)

In the Problem box, do your best to provide a brief but clear summary of the problem. Next, document an outline of the Current State, meaning how things are working today and where breakdowns are happening. Try to outline all of the steps that happen as part of the process today.

The Root Cause section is extremely important. You don't want to create a solution that only deals with the top-level symptoms of a problem; you want to fix it at the true underlying cause—at the root. There are a couple of good tools that are helpful here. The first and easiest is to ask why. When you have a clear picture of what the problem is, an outline of how things are working today, and where the breakdown is, your "why" becomes very powerful. But don't stop with just one why. Ask the question several times:

- "Why is this breakdown happening here?"

- "Because X, Y, and Z."
- "Why are X, Y and Z happening?"
- "Because of A, B and C."
- "Why are A, B and C happening?"

You get the point. The key is to ask this question until you are confident you have found the *root cause* of the problem. That way, when it comes to the proposed solution, you are not just fixing the surface level symptoms. Fix it at the root so it stays fixed. In most cases, by the time you have asked this question five times, you can be confident you are at the root cause. This tool is called "the Five Whys." Fancy, right? Ok, not so fancy but very powerful.

> *The key is to ask this question until you are confident you have found the root cause of the problem.*

If you have a multi-faceted problem, use a "fishbone diagram" (also known as the "cause and effect" diagram). This is another simple but powerful tool that forces you to think through all of the factors that are causing a breakdown in the process.

If you haven't drawn a fishbone lately (or ever), don't worry, just draw something that looks like the head of the fish to one side of the paper. Draw a long line to the other side of the paper and draw a tail. Then draw a few lines toward the top and a few lines toward the bottom, angling away from the head. Add a few horizontal lines to each of those and you've got the start of a good fishbone. The point is to start writing down all of the causes and where they are coming from. Once you have all of the issues written down, you can start to identify the deeper issues.

Next is the ideal state (or how you would like things to be). Without worrying about how things are today, the results you are getting, or the problems you are running into, think about how things would look if everything were just as you would like it to be and write it down. The clearer you can be, the better.

> *Document what needs to happen, who will champion it, and when it should be completed.*

For the Solution section, outline what needs to happen to fix the root causes of your biggest problems and why you think it will be effective. The action section is the proposed implementation plan for the solution. Document what needs to happen, who will champion it, and when it should be completed.

The last two sections are fairly self-explanatory. Outline any Risks you are aware of and how you will tackle them. Then highlight actions that can be taken to make sure you are able to Sustain the improvements made. If possible, Include how you plan to continue to improve even beyond sustaining the current solution.

Once you have taught your team to use the A3 problem-solving methodology, start using it to outline any problem that comes up. If someone brings a problem to you, ask for the A3. This will get your team in the habit of thinking through problems in a structured, systematic, and smart way. It ensures that the problem has been clearly defined, that the current process has been thought through, and that the root cause has been identified before taking action.

I heard the story of one hospital executive who, once he was familiar with this process, used it exclusively. In one corner of his desk he had a one-page summary of every problem that came up. How nice would it be to have that for each of the problems you need to solve?

The leadership equation can be seen within the A3 structure as it contains the current state or where you A̲re today, the ideal state or where you want to B̲e, the root C̲auses of the Challenges and the C̲ountermeasures that are part of the solution and action plan.

Now that you have a structured approach to solving problems, let's looks at how your team members can collaborate on a daily basis to radically increase their effectiveness.

PART 2: PARTS OF THE SYSTEM

CHAPTER 4:

4. THE DAILY HUDDLE

In a typical work scenario, people arrive to work, greet each other, chit-chat, and then start working in their own little world. They might ask each other an occasional question or get together for a moment, but in general it is likely to be random collaboration.

problems that don't get solved quickly tend to grow.

Many workplace cultures inadvertently encourage people to either solve their own problems or pass them off to a manager. When this is the case and someone is having a problem, they are not able to solve, issues tend to fester because they don't get solved quickly. Unfortunately, problems that don't get solved quickly tend to grow.

When I first managed a team, I found that many of the problems brought to me were about two weeks old. Although they had started as small fires, by the time a team member passed them to me, they were big fires. By that point, customers were even more upset than they were in the beginning. Constantly dealing with upset customers is not how you want to spend your time as a leader.

Introduction to the Daily Huddle

The daily huddle is the solution to this problem. The huddle provides a structure and a rhythm for team members to collaborate and for team leaders to tune in to what is going on and support the team as a coach.

If you are familiar with football huddles, this is just a little different. In a football huddle, the quarterback generally relays the play from the coach and confirms that everyone is good to go. Players may provide some quick feedback and or encouragement to other team members. In this huddle, team members take turns facilitating and the focus is on each team member's answers to three questions:

> *What did I do yesterday?*
>
> *What roadblocks am I running into?*
>
> *What am I planning to do today?*

Other team members listen intently to the challenges and provide quick feedback or solutions if possible. If the feedback or related discussion gets too detailed, the facilitator points the conversation to an offline discussion after the meeting, where anyone who has relevant information or ideas can share them with the team member. The meeting lasts no longer than fifteen minutes.

You don't want your meeting to get too big. Huddles should be no larger than twelve people. Anything more than that and the meeting will get too long. If you have a team larger than twelve, consider dividing into multiple huddles.

When I implemented this process with my team, I found that 80 percent of the problems which previously would have been brought to me were solved by other team members. Rather than waiting on me, team members helped each other quickly. The solutions were better than what I would have come up with anyway. This freed up time for me and created a stronger bond between team members.

Fig. 4: The Daily Huddle

Before we jump into how to run the daily huddle, let's walk quickly through preparing the tools you will need to run your daily huddle effectively.

Daily Huddle Preparation Tools

Start by creating a one-page summary that outlines the purpose of the meeting, the process, who needs to be there, where you are going to meet, and at what time.

This summary should only cover this single topic, stay simple, and be kept to one page. Anyone should be able to pick it up and gain a quick understanding of the who, what, when, where, why, and how of the huddle. This type of document is called a "single-point lesson" or SPL.

Be sure to include these components in the SPL:

- An Overview of what the SPL is about
- The Purpose or goals you are trying to accomplish
- Key details about the process being outlined
- The roles and responsibilities / who does what

High-Level Process Map

Once you have a single-point lesson, it's time to create a simple, high-level map of the process for the work you do. Most people are comfortable with following a step-by-step recipe from a cookbook, but when it comes to mapping work related tasks, it might be a little less familiar. The process is actually very much the same. It just takes some getting used to.

If you have not done work-process mapping before, start by practicing with some everyday things such as getting ready in the morning, doing laundry, or making a sandwich. Normally, when you do these things, you don't have to think much about them, but when you try to draw a process map for someone else to follow, you'll have to give it a little more thought.

The sandwich example might look something like this:

- Step 1: lay out two pieces of bread
- Step 2: add the turkey
- Step 3: add the cheese
- Step 4: put mayo on one slice of bread
- Etc.

Fig. 5: High Level Map

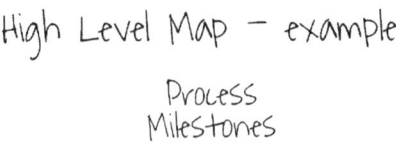

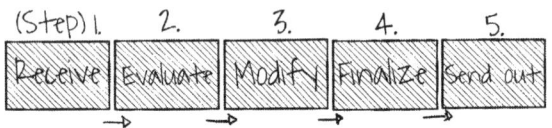

Draw each step in a box with a line pointing to the next step. Keep in mind that these high-level instructions work because we are making certain assumptions (that you have a bag of already sliced bread, etc.). If we wanted to go into more detail, we would have to add additional information:

- Step 1: find the bag of sliced bread
- Step 2: untwist the wire closure mechanism to open the bag
- Step 3: take out two pieces of bread
- Etc.

For now, we want to keep it simple. Maybe the work your team does has twenty-four steps. For this current purpose you should try narrow it down to the major "milestones" of work so you have something closer to a five-to seven-step process.

A good way to figure out the beginning of your process is to ask the question: How do we receive requests for work to be done? (e.g., does an email arrive or does a customer step up to the counter?) The next question is: Then what happens?

By asking these questions and continuing to ask, "then what?" you will end up with a basic map of your overall process. Remember to keep it at a high level and try to identify the major milestones. You will know you are done with your map when you hear something like "and then we deliver it to the customer."

Every work effort has a beginning, a middle, and an end. Mapping out the major milestones of any work effort is not hard to do but most of us don't do it. Either it seems too simple or we just don't bother trying to understand how things actually work.

> *Every work effort has a beginning, a middle, and an end.*

Again, if you haven't done much mapping before, pick an everyday thing that you do like brushing your teeth to practice mapping out your process. Ask the questions, think it through and draw it out. It's that easy.

There are many ways to map a process electronically as well (using Excel, Visio, etc.), but I recommend starting with pencil and paper. If you need share it with others in a different location, just take a picture.

Keep Score to Improve

"If you are not keeping score, you're just practicing."
– Vince Lombardi

A great way to measure performance and identify ways to improve is to find a way to measure the work you do. As part of the daily huddle, you will develop a customized method so that each team member can earn points.

When I first started leading a team, each team member had several projects they were working on and seemed very busy. I could look at the number of projects they were completing over time and have a general sense of what was getting accomplished, but I really had no idea how productive they were on a daily basis. I only knew that something was wrong when a customer would complain.

Finding a good way to measure your work will give you and your team members a much better sense of what is really going on. It also helps you to analyze performance, so you can find ways to improve it. Just like any sporting event, if you are not keeping score, it's hard to know how you are doing or where to focus in order to improve.

An athlete who wants to improve his or her jump or speed must be able to measure current performance in order to record improvement. The same is true for work. And similar to the way each sport has a different type of point system, every type of work must be measured a little differently.

Think about all the ways there are to keep score in different sports: soccer ('futbol'), has one of the simplest systems—one point is earned each time the ball passes into the goal. If a certain type of work is very simple and the same every time, keeping score is going to look like soccer. You can boil the work down to a single point for every effort.

Each game has its own system...

Other work will be more complex like basketball, where a regular basket is worth two points, but if you make a basket from outside the three-point line, you earn three points. And of course, if you are fouled by another player, you shoot "free-throws" that are worth one point each. "American" football has even more different ways to score points.

Each game has its own system and different level of complexity for measuring your efforts and scoring points. The same is true for every different type of work. Therefore, you need to design a customized system for measuring the complexity of the work so that you can score it appropriately.

Once you have the initial layout of points per milestone, it is time to account for the different size and complexity of your work. You do this by thinking back through prior work projects and highlighting the characteristics of different projects that make them require more effort to complete.

Then determine how many different sizes you want to include. For example, you may decide to classify projects as small, medium, or large. If there is a lot of variation in the work that comes to you, then you may want to add extra-large or extra-small, etc. Outline the characteristics of incoming work that you will use to easily determine what size the project will be.

Fig. 10: Milestone Points per Size

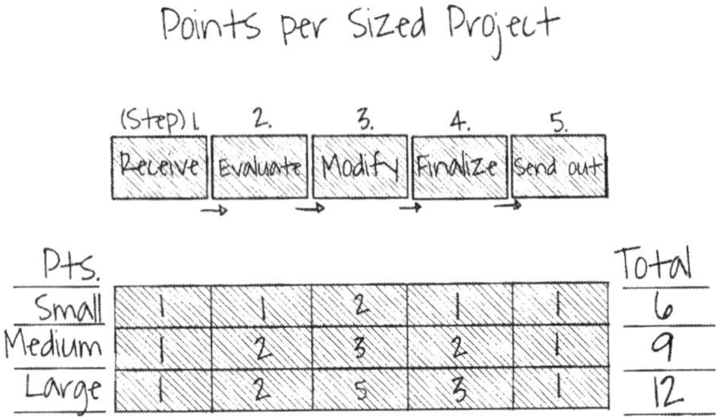

Points per Sized Project

Pts.	(Step) 1. Receive	2. Evaluate	3. Modify	4. Finalize	5. Send out	Total
Small	1	1	2	1	1	6
Medium	1	2	3	2	1	9
Large	1	2	5	3	1	12

All of the information related to the type of work you do, the milestones required to complete it, how each milestone will be scored, and the criteria that will be used to determine the size of the project should be added to a one-page, single-point lesson or Work Points SPL.

Important note: do not use length of time to complete a work effort as a means to measure point value. Ultimately you will find ways to reduce the time it takes (and improve the quality of the work) and you don't want the point value of the work reduced as the time is reduced. Instead, you want to see the amount your productivity has improved due to your improvement efforts.

Once you set up a system to score and measure the work your team does, you can start to set targets for how much work you want to accomplish on a daily basis. These should be stretch targets that are set together with the team. The purpose of the stretch targets is *not* to work harder but to motivate the team to work together and to find ways to work smarter.

Keep in mind that your point system does not need to be perfect in the beginning. You just need something that lets you get started. You will most likely update the measurement system as you gain experience after having tried it out for a while.

At one entry level job I held early in my career, I performed some very boring work. Since it was very easy to count the number of things I was completing and keep score, I kept track in order to stay awake and motivate myself. Every day I would try to complete 200.

At the end of one week on the project, one person had completed almost 1,000 more than me. But when it came time to determine which temps would continue on the project, they determined that the 1,000 plus point person had been going too fast and the quality was very poor.

Make sure that quality is maintained (and improved) as the team works toward their stretch targets. The point of any measurement system is to do the work well, do it consistently and improve in the way you are doing it over time. A good measurement system helps the team to work together to do those things and more.

Here is another look at the different benefits of measuring our work:

- measure the work we do and find ways to improve
- compare the work required for different sized projects or different milestones
- measure the amount of "work output" or "productivity" in a way that is different than just measuring the number of projects completed
- increase team member and manager knowledge / visibility to all work
- increase accountability for actual work results among team members
- share best practices
- provide a self-motivation tool
- create a more robust environment for identification of roadblocks, team collaboration, and the identification of process improvement opportunities

Work points are part of the process focused effort to improve the work we do to reach a sustainable speed of production and level of quality. In addition to measuring work so you can keep score, you need an easy way to look up and see what is going on without having to ask a lot of questions or run reports—you need a scoreboard.

Visual Management Tools

The Huddle Support "Scoreboard"

Gathering regularly for structured collaboration and accountability in the daily huddle is a big step in the right direction. Adding a method for appropriately measuring the work you do so you can keep score takes you to the next level. To maximize the benefit of both these initial steps and create a high-performing team, you need to add an element of visual management by creating a scoreboard. This can also be referred to as a huddle support board.

If you ask most managers or leaders how their team is doing, they will likely need to get back to you while they go back to their desk to try to run some reports or review recent customer feedback surveys, etc.

A visual management scoreboard allows you to look up and see what is going on with the part of your business that you are responsible for at any time. With this scoreboard you can see what each team member is working on, how they are doing, and how the team is doing overall in terms of managing the amount of incoming work that needs to be done and any targets that have been set related to work completion.

Have you ever been to a sporting event or watched one on TV and not seen a scoreboard? All games have some form of a scoreboard. Work is the same: you need a scoreboard.

The main difference between a visual management scoreboard for work and the scoreboard for most sports contests is that you are not competing against another team but rather against the total amount of work that needs to be completed and any targets that you have set related to work completion. The board also supports the huddle by providing a place to capture the challenges that are discussed as well as improvement ideas.

The scoreboard provides something concrete that will both facilitate discussion and make it clear how your team is really doing, what the challenges are, and how close they are to their targets. When these are clear for all to see, it helps everyone to keep moving in the same direction.

How to Create Your Huddle Support "Scoreboard"

To create your team scoreboard, invite the team to a board-building team exercise. Prepare the materials and templates in advance. During the meeting, divide the team up into two groups. The first group can use the black art tape to outline the different sections of the board. The second group can use a label maker machine to print out the headers for the board and all of the different sections.

Start with a dry-erase white board around three-feet tall by four-feet wide. It is ok to use a different size, but this is a good starting point and fairly easy to find at a local office supply store. If you already have something similar that is a different size, feel free to use what you have.

Fig. 11: The Huddle Support Board

Huddle Support Board

Facilitator	* Daily Target					Week	Priorities
Team Members	*	M	T	W	T	F	Impediments	
Superman								Follow-ups
Batman								
Wonder Woman								
Aquaman								
							Team Impediments	Improvements/Innovations
Team Target								
Total								

Divide the scoreboard according to your template using the thin black art tape. On the left side, you will list team members and keep track of the points they earned related to the work they accomplished. In the middle list the roadblocks that team members are running into. The right side is for capturing important areas of focus, improvement ideas, and innovation ideas.

In most cases, teams chose avatar names or code names to list on the scoreboard instead of real names. This ensures that no one will be publicly embarrassed if they don't hit their targets. For some people and for some cultures, the fear of publicly not hitting a target is a really big deal.

Teams tend to enjoy this part of the process as they get to choose an alter-ego of sorts. If you want to be He-Man on the support board, you can be He-Man. You want accountability within the team, but you also want safety. Otherwise team members may cut corners in order to hit targets, which reduces the quality of your work.

Before the daily huddle starts, team members write their points from the prior day on the left side of the board. As the meeting takes place, team members or the facilitator capture roadblocks as well as improvement and innovation ideas. The team leader can use the upper right corner to highlight important updates or areas of focus.

It is helpful to remember the setup of the board like this: the right-hand side is the more free-thinking, creative side whereas the left-hand side is where you keep track of the hard numbers related to the work being done. This is similar in a way to our "left brain" and "right brain." In between the two, you have team member's roadblocks or challenges.

The scoreboard provides a visual tool that everyone can reference, which shows how the team is doing, the challenges people are facing, the top priorities, ideas for improvement, and innovation ideas. This is an extremely powerful team management tool.

> *Have you ever been to a sporting event or watched one on TV and not seen a scoreboard?*

You may run into questions about what constitutes innovation versus an improvement. There is a very close relationship between improvement and innovation, but innovation generally takes things a step further. The important thing is that you capture the idea!

Ideas for improvement and innovation may also be related to team morale or the work environment in general.

The Project Support Board

There is another great tool for keeping track of all the projects that are going on at any given time—the project support board. Whereas the huddle support board shows how the team is doing, the project support board provides a quick and easy view of all the projects that are in the process and how balanced the work is across the team.

If the type of work you do is "in-and-out" quick turnaround work and team members complete more than ten different work efforts per day you probably don't need this board—you can skip this part or simply modify it in a way that suits your needs. If your team completes one project over several days or works on multiple projects that are in different stages, this tool is extremely valuable as it helps to manage your team's work visually, i.e. "visual management".

The basic template for the project support board lists the team members avatar names down the left-hand side and the major process milestones across the top from left to right. Leave a column space to the left of the names for any inventory of projects that have not been assigned to a team member. Add an extra column at the bottom of the board for STAT or emergency projects.

Instead of a dry-erase white board, use large white project paper approximately four-feet tall by eight-feet wide. If you have access to an extra-large paper printer, that works best. Otherwise, make do with bulletin board paper or project paper that can be found at local office supply stores.

Assign each size project a sticky note color. For example, small projects might be yellow, medium projects green, and large projects blue, etc. Write the project name and pertinent details on the sticky note. As a team member completes steps of work, the sticky note is moved to the appropriate milestone. By doing this, you and your team members have an extremely valuable picture of all the work that is currently in process by the team as well as a very good sense of what the priorities are and who might have some additional bandwidth for special projects.

If any customer (internal or external) were to ask you where the project was, you could simply go to the board and look. For internal customers, you could invite them to the board, explain the process, and help them find their project. Then, the next time they have a question, guess what? They don't even need to ask you! And if they ask why their project isn't complete yet, you can look at both boards to see any challenges going on and the workload of the team member to identify a very real answer.

You also now have the capability to do workload balancing. If you see that one team member has a light amount of work in progress and another team member is clearly overloaded and there is a similar skill set, you can shift some of the work so that you have a more balanced workload across team members.

Fig. 13: Project Support Board

Team Member	Major Milestones					Completed Work
	1	2	3	4	5	
~~	▫▫	▫	▫▫ ▫	▫		
~~	▫	▫▫	▫▫	▫	▫	

Combined, the huddle support board and the project support board help to visualize the work that is going on when discussing the three questions during the daily huddle. When a team member answers what they did yesterday, they can point to the board to show their point totals and the related challenges they are having (the second question), as well as where each of their initiatives are in the process of completion on the project support board and what they are planning to do today.

Team Data Log

"Captains log, star-date 41153.5, today we are headed for planet Domoor IV..."

Just like the captain of the Starship Enterprise in the movie *Star Trek*, you need to regularly record what is going on with your team. Although you may not hit a button and speak it yet, don't worry, I'm sure that is coming soon... "Siri Alexa, yesterday the team total points were..." For now, capture the data from the huddle support board and the project support board in a team data log spreadsheet so that nothing is lost. The team data log should include:

- A schedule of rotating responsibilities and who owns them each week
- A list of all incoming work (this is likely kept in a separate software—listing it here as a reminder that it is important to have somewhere)
- The team's weekly performance and point totals for each team member

- A list of the problems brought up and any solutions (acts as a great FAQ doc)
- An improvement plan which includes a prioritized list of all improvement ideas

At the end of the week, prior to erasing the board, the facilitator should update the team data log with the point totals for the team as well as all impediments identified and resolved. Everything that was on the board gets captured in this log, so you never lose information. Even resolved problems are moved from the board to log. Once they are captured in the log, then it is fine to erase them from the board.

Remember—team members keep track of their own points via the honor system and put them on the board. The facilitator transfers information from the board to the log. Setting up this system cannot be about adding additional work for the team leader. It is about clarifying roles and then sharing leadership responsibilities so that team members gain experience and grow in their capabilities.

Conducting the Daily Huddle

To kick off the daily huddle, prepare a couple of slides that review the purpose, process, tools and basic guidelines. Do a dry run using these slides with team managers (depending on how your team is structured) before getting together with the team to make sure that everything is clearly laid out. Schedule a meeting with the team and go over the slides, leaving time for questions at the end.

Expect questions during the kickoff meeting. Be glad there are questions even if they seem negative. In your response, focus on why the team is doing this: to improve performance and grow in our capabilities as individuals and as a team. Conclude the meeting by confirming the date (ideally the following Monday) you will start doing the daily huddle.

A good huddle will be short and high energy. It will also feel supportive but self-managed. Remind team members of this as you get started.

Your huddle should start as early in the day as possible but only after all team members are present or available (you may have some remote members who join via phone).

Apply the principle of respect here. That means that you should start the huddle on-time and end on-time because you are being respectful of people and their time.

On the agreed start day, everyone stands for the huddle in a circle or semi-circle at the place and time you've determined to meet. For the first week, the team leader should facilitate the meeting to provide an example of how it works. Then facilitation rotates among team members on a weekly basis and the team leader is no longer part of the rotation.

The facilitator initiates the meeting by choosing someone to begin and keeps the meeting on track. Each team member (including the facilitator) answers the three questions (what I did yesterday, what roadblocks I am running into, and what I am planning to do today) and provides relevant ideas for the roadblocks of other team members. Team members report out to each other and not the team leader.

The team should focus on the 2nd and 3rd questions more than the 1st one. Avoid storytelling so that the meeting keeps moving forward. As the roadblocks and relevant ideas are presented, they can be added to the scoreboard by the team member or the facilitator. Any lengthy discussions should be taken off-line after the huddle. Team members should be able to point quickly to the project support board when mentioning specific projects and the huddle support board when talking about their daily point total.

At the end of the meeting, the facilitator asks if the team leader has any questions or comments. If any problems or ideas were brought up during the meeting that need more discussion, smaller groups can get together after the huddle is finished.

The changeover process to the next facilitator happens after the Monday morning huddle because during this huddle you are reviewing the numbers from Friday's work on the huddle support board. The current facilitator can take a picture of the board after the meeting in order to transfer the results to the team log.

Benefits of the Daily Huddle

On the surface, this basic concept of the structured huddle is extremely simple, but the results can be profound.

Look at all the things that are happening just below the surface:

- Team members are standing up and "presenting" to a small group—practicing the leadership skill of public speaking.
- Each team member takes on the facilitation role and leads this small meeting which acts as a confidence builder to leading larger gatherings in the future.
- By sharing the challenges they are facing, team members are being vulnerable which builds trust because it requires trust.
- Team members share what they did and what they are planning to do, which provides accountability.
- Team members are helping to solve problems encountered by their peers which is a benefit to those that are helped and to those whose confidence level is raised because they are helping—creating a stronger bond between team members.
- Issues that can't be solved by a fellow team member escalate to the team leader. This acts as a built-in filtration process because only the problems that really need your help are presented to you.
- Issues are brought up quickly, which keeps them from becoming bigger issues. It is always easier to put out a small fire rather than a large one.

Are you starting to see the incredible benefits? Here is a common pushback I hear to this process: We are so busy; we just don't have time to take fifteen minutes out of our day to meet like this; it's a burden to our team members and they just really don't want to do it.

This is where smart leadership comes in. You don't have time to *not* do this. If you don't have a system like this in place, multiple team members will stop you in the hallway or at your desk for a "two-minute" question. Of course, they are never two-minute questions. And 80 percent of them could have been solved by someone else on your team other than you.

As a leader, you are maximizing the benefit of the team's collaboration by empowering team members to provide solutions rather than just looking to you as the focal point of issue resolution.

Some issues will require your involvement to solve. This process gives you visibility to see the issues quickly before they have time to grow into issues which take a large amount of your time and effort.

The structure of the huddle allows leaders and managers to be more strategic in the overall management of the work and act as a supportive coach to team members rather than just react to problems.

How Much Work Can Our Team Do?

The history of weekly team point totals gives you the data you need for the beginning of your "productivity model," i.e., a mathematical equation, that shows how much work can be completed by your team over a given time period.

If you know that the volume of work is going to increase and the requirement from customers for the turn-around time is a certain number of days, you will know how many team members are needed to keep up with expectations and whether you can keep up with demand at your current team size.

Without this type of model, if your work volume goes up but your team size and turn-around time from customers stays the same, you are likely to end up with upset customers, because their requests will take longer than they have in the past. This can cause some major issues. Especially if, as a leader, you are unable to understand and explain why things are taking longer with numbers to back up what you are saying.

By creating a productivity model and capturing the data for roadblocks and resolutions as well as improvement and innovation ideas, you have created some very powerful information:

Clear understanding of current team performance and the basis for a productivity model (i.e., understanding how much work your team can complete)

Have a problem? Check the roadblocks and resolutions list to see if anyone has run into the same problem in the past and what they did about it

The list of improvement ideas can be evaluated, prioritized, and assigned champions. Just add dates for desired completion to selected initiatives, and you have the beginning of a solid project plan for improvement!

The Daily Huddle Recipe Book

The "ingredients" you will need for your daily huddle:
- ~3x4 dry-erase white board
- 1/8-inch black art tape (find online)
- Label maker
- Scissors
- Tape measure / yard stick
- A spreadsheet (Excel or Google Sheets, Numbers, etc.)
- Blank slides (PowerPoint, Google Slides, Keynote, etc.)
- Word processing document (Word, Google Docs, Pages, etc.)

The steps to follow to make it happen (checklist):
- Develop standard daily huddle single-point lesson (SPL)
- Create a high-level map of the major milestones of your work
- Develop a Work Points SPL with points assigned to each milestone for each size project
- Conduct a scoreboard building exercise with the team
    - Order white board (~3'x4')
    - Develop a template according to your team size
    - Conduct an exercise with the team to build the board (apply lines and labels according to template created)

- - Install board at daily huddle location on a wall or a tripod
- Conduct kick off meeting with team
  - Develop kick off meeting slides
  - Do a dry run with managers
  - Conduct kick off meeting
- Launch daily huddle
  - Launch the daily huddle according to your single-point lesson guide
- Develop daily data collection and roadblock resolution process
  - Develop white board data capture template
  - Develop template for roadblock list and resolution process

Easy Peasy Lemon Squeezy

"In the beginning, you just need to be 60 percent confident." - Coach K

Do not worry about being 100 percent right and get stalled by indecision. Just be 60 percent confident which will allow you to move forward. Then you can modify things as you move along in the process.

The daily huddle is a mechanism for collaboration, feedback, learning and encouragement. The huddle works whether you are standing next to the person or they are halfway around the world.

It is an incredibly easy process to get going and it helps the team to get organized and to start collaborating, problem solving, and learning from each other in addition to holding each other accountable.

Now, you might be thinking, "My team is different—we don't fit this mold." Maybe you don't see each other every day or maybe each shift has different team members. The way the huddle is laid out here is one way to do it. Take the core concepts—shared problem-solving, shared accountability, shared facilitation, and the three focus questions and find a way to make them work for your team. For example, if you don't meet regularly, maybe your questions change to:

1.) What have I been working on?

2.) What challenges am I running into?

3.) What am I planning to do next?

These questions work no matter how frequently you get together.

The daily huddle sets the stage for the next phase of the system, the weekly game plan.

Chapter 5

5. THE WEEKLY GAME PLAN

"The first step to getting somewhere is to decide that you are not going to stay where you are."

- J.P. Morgan

Most people don't get excited about meetings because they are frequently inefficient, unproductive, boring, and people fall asleep (I've done it myself, and I've had people fall asleep in my meetings prior to using this system).

This meeting is different because it is structured in a way that requires team members to actively participate—no one just sits there passively taking notes. Like a football or basketball game, the hour-long, weekly team meeting is divided into four quarters:

- Quarter 1: Manager update and team performance review
- Quarter 2: Process improvement review of ideas and projects in process
- Quarter 3: Team member teaches a topic of value
- Quarter 4: Celebrations, events, and recognition

The planning, preparation, structure, and most of all the sharing of leadership duties creates effective meetings. Set up a schedule that shows which team member owns each duty listed in the leadership duties section for the next meeting. (see the leadership duties listed below.)

The data needed for the manager update and team performance review flows out of the collection of data from the daily huddle. And all members share the responsibility for taking the data and putting it into presentation form.

The manager goes through the process first to ensure the directions are clear and everything works as it should. In this way, the manager models the process, trains others to lead, and then coaches them as they lead. Although this may seem small, this process of modeling, giving responsibility, and then coaching makes a huge difference.

Does this mean that team members don't have a little bit of creative license to go beyond what is expected for their responsibilities? Absolutely not. You would be amazed at the creativity that team members added to our weekly meeting presentations.

From fancy slide changes to funny content to additional information about what was going on in the workplace and in the community (during the rewards and recognition section), it was awesome! And it was valuable to team members—it kept them engaged, and the creators felt proud. We usually left meetings feeling good, invigorated to move forward, and with smiles on our faces. Is that the way you leave meetings now?

During each quarter of the meeting, after reviewing the information or ideas, you should have some discussion. If you are simply plodding through information or "getting through the chapter" as some of my teachers used to say in school, you are missing a huge opportunity.

The purpose of reviewing the information is not actually to review information.

The purpose is to gain understanding, generate discussion, clarify ideas, and be ready to move forward in a better way with what you are doing. If you don't do this as part of the time where you are together, you are missing it! Don't miss it!

Leadership Roles

See the leadership roles listed below. Keep in mind that you will create a short, single-point lesson to go along with each one of these, which will include the customized details that are specific to your team.

Leadership Role 1: Overall responsibility for organizing the meeting, scheduling the meeting, and gathering slides from other team members to put into a presentation.

Leadership Role 2: Team performance update; gather the data from the huddle meeting log, put it into a chart, analyze it, and put the chart and commentary into a slide for the presentation.

Leadership Role 3: Look at the improvement plan and put it into a slide. Lead the discussion and update the slide with details from the discussion.

Leadership Role 4: Provide training for the team on a selected area of expertise.

Leadership Role 5: Reward and recognition. Gather kudos and recognition from team members and the team leader to be placed into slides. Include any additional information provided by team members about things they are doing in the community, events, etc. The team leader may also add recognition.

But wait! What do I do as the leader if all of these leadership roles are being done by team members? You get to truly lead. How? You will not be bogged down with the details or trying to do it all on your own. You will be able to think strategically, and you will be able to coach—guiding team members and encouraging and recognizing team members.

Also, don't forget that at the very beginning of the meeting, prior to jumping into the performance data, you should provide a quick leader / manager update.

Benefits of the Meeting

Let's look at a typical meeting prep scenario with no system in place:

The manager prepares an agenda and then scrambles to put together some data that gives a sense of the team's performance. If any of the leadership responsibility is shared, they assign it at the last minute and without much instruction or guidance. "I'm too busy right now; just figure it out!" Then, during the meeting, the hastily-prepared results are force-fed to a bored team with a few frustrated people fuming over being "delegated" tasks at the last minute without much instruction. Not the best!

Instead, with this system, team members:

- Know their responsibilities ahead of time (see sample responsibilities chart)
- Know the directions as they clearly state how to do what needs to be done
- don't spend too much time away from normal tasks
- receive recognition for their efforts
- build up their leadership capabilities
- are involved in the process, and, therefore, are engaged
- know what to expect and how the meeting will flow

Fig. 17: Weekly Game Plan slides

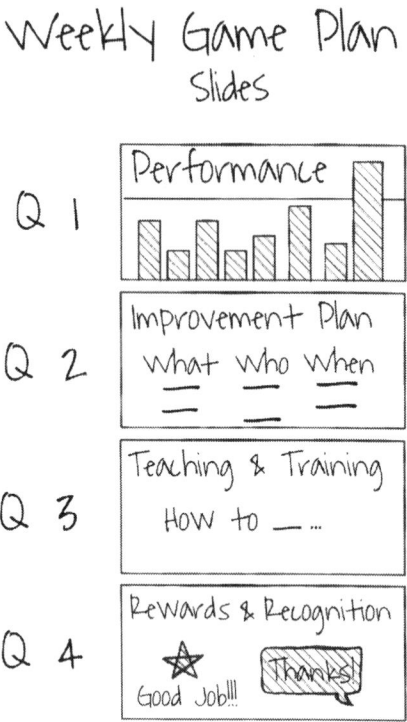

(Download FREE templates at:
THELEADERSHIPFORMULABOOK.com)

First Quarter of the Meeting: Manager Update and Performance Review

The meeting starts with the leader or manager update: things that you, as the leader, may be aware of that the team is not yet, updates from customer meetings, etc. This is the stuff that other leaders will try to create entire meetings out of and the reason people are disengaged and fall asleep. You will be able to knock it out in a few minutes. When it is short and sweet, it becomes valuable information that is being shared with the team; keeping them up to date rather than boring them.

Then, you want to look at the weekly team totals over time. Wait to start this meeting until you had a couple of months of daily huddle data under your belt, so you can look at the data and create bar charts that show the results and the related trend. Are the team totals going up or down?

Importantly, you can analyze the data and provide commentary in addition to the numbers. Because you have already captured this info as part of recording the results of the huddle, this is easy to do.

You may need to "normalize" your targets by adjusting for any absent team members or accepted interruptions to either the number of hours available to get work done or the amount of people at work. Your data will tell you this information. Was someone out on vacation last week or did you have two days of required team training for a new software being implemented? Let's say, for example, your team point target for the week is typically 250 points per week (ten per day x five team members x five days), but you did have two days where the entire team was pulled out for required training, you would need to adjust your target down by 100 (ten per day x five team members x two days).

Then, add other information from the capture of the daily data: large roadblocks or reasons for spikes in productivity, etc. At the bottom of the chart, add other key information related to client requests or any other additional information. Again, the total time allotted for this section is fifteen minutes—enough to give a quick update, review the data, analyze the trends, and discuss the results.

During the data review, you want everyone to get in the habit of reviewing their work results *and* recognizing that their effort is part of a team effort, reinforcing they are not just getting work done but they are a part of a team.

When you are part of a team, you feel more drive to pull your weight, you have the opportunity to give to other team members by helping to solve problems, provide training, etc., and you receive support and feedback from other team members. This helps people to grow which is a need that most of us have in order to feel satisfied. Being part of a well-organized team increases individual satisfaction which in turn increases team performance.

Quarter Two of the Meeting: The Improvement Plan

The improvement plan initially comes directly from the log developed while you were setting up your daily huddle. But don't stop there. Add ideas as they come up. When it comes time to review the list during the meeting, your goal is to refine and prioritize the ideas.

Discuss each improvement idea with the team. Gain a better understanding of the pain point that caused this improvement idea in the first place. How big is the pain? How widespread is it (does it affect everyone)? How frequently does it happen? Is it so bad that even customers know that it is a challenge for your team? The sum total of these questions should give you an overall sense of the severity and urgency of the problem. Write some notes about it and give it an overall impact rating using a one to ten rating system or whatever works best for you.

Ok, we're through the second quarter. Start your halftime show! Or just get up and do some jumping jacks if you want but only take a short break to make sure that the team member doing the training for the next quarter is all set to go. This should not be more than two to three minutes. You don't want people drifting into long side conversations that make it hard to refocus. The next quarter is an important moment for the team member doing the training.

Quarter Three of the Meeting: Peer-to-Peer Training

You've reviewed performance and talked about how to improve, now it is time to "level-up" the skills of your team members. In some cases, this scheduled training will be directly related to an improvement area identified in the past. In other cases, it will be based on a general area of improvement or a particularly valuable skill that a team member can share.

The trainer should prepare two to three slides, give or take, including an outline of what they will be training on and screenshots of the process, especially if it is software related. The training should last about ten minutes with time for Q and A at the end. These peer-to-peer training bursts are not intended to be your entire training program. They should supplement other, regular training and are a good way to keep skills up to date.

Frequently training programs try to do all the training for new team members when they first start on the job. After that, they are pretty much on their own. If you want to see your team members continue to grow and improve in the work they do, not to mention be satisfied because they are learning and growing, you need to have a system for regular training and learning.

Quarter Four of the Meeting:
Rewards, Recognition, and Celebration
(It's Party Time!)

The team member responsible for this section solicits input from the team beforehand and then shares with the group. Most people receive compliments or a "thank you" from customers that are easy to cut and paste into a presentation slide.

In addition to work related recognition, team members can share things they have done in the community: volunteer activities, charity runs; or things they have done with their family, like building a new house or a great vacation they took. This sharing continues the bonding experience for team members. Team members who know each other and celebrate with each other, generally work better together, even when things get tough.

Recognize and celebrate the work and personal accomplishments of team members and the team. Sharing compliments publicly and celebrating successes with everyone can have a compounding, positive impact. Most times, a team member gets to enjoy this recognition once and maybe twice if they forward it on to the manager or team leader. Here you get to give those good feelings the full light of day. They are spoken about at a meeting and the team member gets to feel good multiple times because they are being recognized and applauded by the entire team. Like a pig in mud, sometimes you just need to rub around in that stuff for a while.

Are you starting to see the *huge* amount of value that you can gain from a one-hour meeting one time per week that is done right? All kinds of good things happen: leadership skills are practiced, planning for the future, training and learning, sharing, recognizing and celebrating. These are the things that make a great team!

CHAPTER 6

6. MONTHLY IMPROVEMENT EVENTS

Let's review what you've done so far as it sets the stage for what comes next:

- Taught your team members a structured approach to problem solving, empowered them with the permission to solve problems
- Set up your team to collaborate on the early identification and quick resolution of problems and share accountability for getting things done
- Created a high-level map of the major milestones of your overall process
- Found a way to measure the work that you do so you can put numbers on the scoreboard / support board and measure daily productivity

- Created a schedule so the system is not dependent on any one person or leader to keep things moving and organized

Introduction to
Monthly Improvement Events

Now it is time to incorporate an event that requires a little more time and that pays huge dividends. Once a month, the key stakeholders for your group or company should gather together for an entire day or two and strategize, in a very structured way, how to improve.

What to focus on during this event should flow from the improvement plans that are reviewed during the weekly meetings or will come directly from a customer or company leader.

There are four main parts to this type of event. If you do them all, the event will be fairly simple and extremely valuable. If you skip one (like the planning or the post event follow-up), it will be a waste of your time—so don't skimp!

The average amount of time required to conduct an event like this is about a day and a half. It is possible to complete them quicker, and certainly you can take an entire week or more if you really wanted to, but in general about two days is the right amount of time to really be effective. If you are doing them regularly, you will become proficient enough that a single day will be sufficient.

If the scope of what you are trying to solve is much bigger and will require more time, then use an initial session to break it up into more manageable chunks and then conduct separate events where you can dig deeper and focus better on the specific areas.

Don't let the idea of a larger event with bigger problems and more people scare you. These can be really simple and extremely effective, as long as you have a plan and you follow your plan.

Here are the five simple steps you can follow to run a process improvement event:

- Plan and do the pre-work
- Prepare the room
- Present and facilitate discussion
- Document the decisions
- Post event follow-ups and follow-throughs

Another good way to think about it is: Think - Plan - Prepare - Execute – Evaluate – Follow-up.

This can be helpful if you tend to get stuck in the thinking stage. Sometimes people try to go right from thinking to executing and forget about the planning and preparation. It doesn't work! Be aware of this and make sure you move into the planning stage. I know because I've tried to do it. You have to take time to plan and prepare if you want it to go well.

Think, Plan and Do the Pre-Work

Prepare A3 documents

Proposal A3

You are already familiar with the problem-solving A3 which guides you through the problem-solving process and provides an easy way to share that process with others—improving your results. Now let's look at another way to use the structure and simplicity of the A3 format so that you can move out of the thinking stage and start planning.

A Proposal A3 is just a little different than a Problem-Solving A3 in that it includes information about the event and the team needed to address the issue. This document captures an overall summary of what the problem is, what you are trying to accomplish, who the stakeholders are, and the desired outcome. The purpose of the proposal A3 is to gain buy-in and sign-off as needed from any key leaders. It is an excellent document for communication as it tells the story of the problem in succinct form.

Fig. 18: Proposal A3

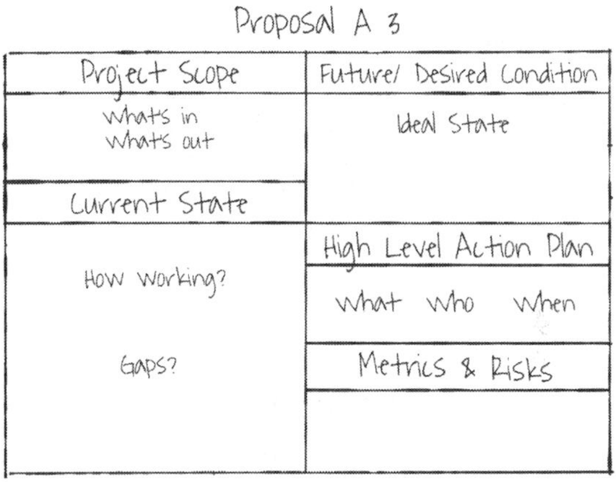

Proposal A 3

Project Scope	Future/ Desired Condition
What's in What's out	Ideal State
Current State	
How working?	High Level Action Plan
	What Who When
Gaps?	Metrics & Risks

Keep in mind that the story doesn't have to be perfect. For now, "just good enough" will do. This is also a good time to consider the financial implications of fixing this problem for your team or your company.

Strategy A3

It is important to remember that the documents you are using are working documents—they are intended to help you think through the process, not act as some formality or fluff for publication or check-the-box procedure. They are "living, breathing" documents and should continue to change as your thinking and understanding does. This is also not something that you have to do perfectly.

Some people don't do it because they don't have all the answers. Instead, get started with what you do have and fill in the rest as you go along.

Once you gain the needed buy-in with the Proposal A3, create a Strategy A3 for your own planning. In addition to the general overview of the problem, the purpose of the Strategy A3 is to add the details about what needs to be done, how it should be done, and the initial agenda for the event. The Strategy A3 is useful for planning for the event and internal team communication.

The Strategy A3 includes: the scope, current state, proposed strategy, a list of stakeholders and a schedule of where and when you will gather for the event.

Fig. 19: Strategy A3

Scope	Proposed Strategy	Stakeholders/ Team Members
What is being considered/included?	Strategy	Who
Current State		
How is it working? How is it not?	Tentative agenda	Schedule
	Deliverables	Where When

Problem-Solving A3

We discussed how to create this in chapter 3. The problem-solving A3 adds an initial dive into the root cause of the problem itself. This is important! Even if a potential solution has been outlined, if the root cause of the problem is not fully understood, then we will likely never reach the desired state because we will not be able to successfully navigate the terrain between where we are today and where we want to be.

(Download FREE templates at:
THELEADERSHIPFORMULABOOK.com)

Prepare and Send Your Map to Key Stakeholders for Completion

Once your A3s are complete, you should be ready to develop a high-level process map. The process steps or milestones from the Current State section of the A3 development process should now be transferred to a spreadsheet mapping document so it can be distributed to the key stakeholders to fill in the additional details. Ask them to add the major milestones of the work they do as well as the more detailed process steps from their unique perspective, related pain points, and any improvement ideas. Depending on how relevant they are to the process, you may want to also include tools that are used and any databases that are referenced for the process.

Whether or not you have very little info (and are basically sending a blank template) or you have a good initial map and you are simply asking team members to validate the information you have and add their pain points and improvement ideas, this needs to be sent out to the team with a deadline for them to get it back to you with their added information. Afterwards, it can be consolidated in preparation for the live event.

The last preparation piece is to formulate the initial agenda for the event. A sample is below, and this can be modified as appropriate, depending on the size of the team, the size of the problem, how much time you will have together, etc.

Fig. 22: Improvement Event Agenda Example

Proposed Improvement Event Agenda

- Kick-Off
    - Introductions
    - Level Set – Why we are here
    - Leadership expectations
- Summary of A3 (Problem Definition, Scope etc.) – 3 to 4 slides
    - Scope
    - Current State Process and Data (results)
    - Gaps / challenges
    - Expected deliverables
- Optional – Key Challenges / Venting exercise
    - 1/2 hour – list per team
- Develop Value Statement
    - Process to address challenges / becomes "true north" to cross-check processes against
- Group Session – Review of current state by teams
    - Process & Results
- Break-out session (will vary based on the scope of project and size of group)
    - Review map from beginning to end – all the way to the customer
    - Review all pain points provided in pre-work; team will discuss and provide solutions
- Teams Report Out
- Improvement Project Plan developed
    - Prioritized improvement ideas with owners and timeline
- Improvement Event Follow-up
    - Governance (leadership owners)
    - Teams & Objectives
    - Regular meeting and reporting cadence

Once you have the Problem-Solving A3, the map with feedback from participants, and an agenda for the event, email these to all the participants. Also, make sure that participants confirm their attendance (and make travel arrangements as necessary).

Finalize the Agenda

Take your initial agenda plus any feedback you receive from stakeholders and finalize it. You may need to be flexible as you get into the event but having a firm agenda will give you the confidence to do so. Depending on the size of your team and the length of your event, your agenda and how much time you are able to spend on each activity will vary. Below is an example agenda that is good for a standard one or two-day event. No matter what length of time you have available, you will still want to use a customized version of this so that you are sure to accomplish the unique goals related to your event. Either way, this is a great starting place.

- Kick Off: Welcome by facilitator and review any housekeeping (coffee and restrooms are usually top priority!)
- Introductions around the room (who you are and what you do)
- Key stakeholder or senior company leader (if available) to thank everyone for being here and highlight the importance of the issue / opportunity
- Review the A3: problem definition, current state, etc. (in a presentation slide). If possible, this is best done by the person who has primary ownership of the area being discussed.
- Optional "venting" / key challenges exercise using giant sticky note pads on an easel (here you simply ask everyone to state the biggest challenges related to the process being discussed).
- Develop value statement which becomes the "true north" or goal for the team—what does the "promised land"/ideal state look like after this is finished?

- Review the giant process map that is on the wall as a team: walk through the major milestones of the current state. This helps everyone to wrap their mind around the full scope of what is being analyzed.
- Group sessions: divide into teams to review sections of the process map and confirm or update as necessary—also discuss proposed improvement ideas, add any new ideas.
- As the map is updated, someone must update the original electronic version as well. Assign this duty to someone other than the facilitator prior to the event.
- Main group: spokesperson from each team reports out on the map, the pain points, and the proposed solutions for the part of the process that they are responsible for.
- Check to see if each of the pain points has been addressed by at least one improvement idea. Also, take the time necessary to get to the root cause of any pain point that seems to be a surface-level issue before determining the path to improvement.
- As teams are reporting out, make sure that someone is capturing this information as this is the beginning of the improvement plan that will be developed next.
- Develop the improvement plan: Prioritize the list of improvement initiatives with the team to create an improvement plan based on the work done so far. Add someone to be the champion (frequently the person who owns the related process step or the person who came up with the improvement idea) and potential

team members for each initiative as well as an estimated date for completion.
- As you discuss each initiative, the champion and others will help identify a realistic timeline for completion while recognizing that there may be some external circumstances that influence the timeline. For example, someone may say, "If we don't have this done by February 6, we are going to lose X customer!" If you want to keep X customer, then that may become your default date for completion of that initiative.

Fig. 23: Improvement Action Plan

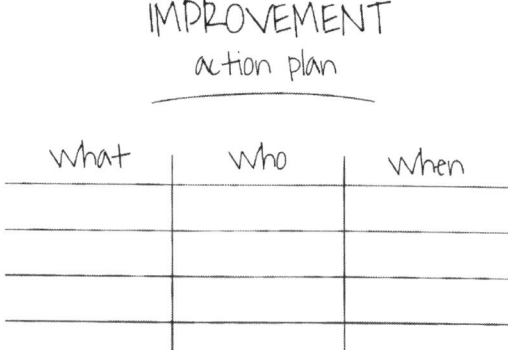

- Some of the improvement ideas brought up may be so simple that they are "Do Now" or "Stop Now" type of initiatives. These can be labeled as such but should still have a champion so that it is clear who will be responsible to make sure that it happens (or stops happening). You also may come up with some ideas that fall outside the scope of your current focus—put these into a "Parking Lot" list to be reviewed at another time.

- Governance of the improvement plan: Close the live event by walking through what happens next. You now have a good improvement plan that is based on the detailed process map with pain points and improvement ideas that address root causes. Each prioritized improvement initiative on the plan needs a champion and a timeline.
- Talk through how frequently the champions of each initiative will be getting together via conference call or in person to provide a status update and who will be the "governance team" (usually the champions and any other key leaders or interested parties) to hear those updates and provide support and feedback.
- Meeting Recap and Close: Using your introduction slides plus the agenda and the action plan, walk through a recap of everything that has happened leading up to getting together, during the meeting and then what will happen after. If possible have a senior leader return to hear the report out, thank everyone for their participation, and re-emphasize how important this initiative is to the company. If a senior leader cannot attend the closing, simply walk through a recap of the agenda and what will happen next.

Prepare the Room

The main part of prepping the room is to take the map with everyone's input and consolidate all the feedback into one larger-than-life document to go on the wall. This may require a day or so to prepare.

The best way to do this is to buy a large roll of bulletin board or project paper from an office supply store (not all stores have it, so you may want to call ahead or look online) that will be used in conjunction with "wall-mount" strips that can be easily removed afterwards to provide a working surface on the wall. Then use yellow, red, and green large and medium sized sticky notes to outline everything from your consolidated map document and put it on the wall.

Use a Sharpie or dry-erase marker to write the major process milestone on the large sticky note so it is easy to read. Use the medium sized sticky notes (yellow is a good color for this) to fill in the process details below each major milestone.

Remember that you are mapping the process as it happens currently (rather than how you want it to be in the future) so that you can have a productive discussion with the team based on how things work today.

Another perspective that can be added later is to focus on the future state (where you want to be) and the initiatives that must be completed to get there. This is valuable to do if you have time. However, don't make the mistake of jumping directly to the ideal future state without analyzing where you are today. Otherwise, you may miss some critical steps and end up stuck with your current process. Remember, it is hard to draw a clear map to 'B' if you don't have a good understanding of 'A'.

Add red sticky notes with pain points and the green sticky notes with improvement ideas below the process step they are related to. When you are done with this you are going to have a good-looking map that is going to facilitate your discussion during the live event. Again, this is a very important visual and is the main preparation of the room.

Documentation and Decision Making

During the event, a team member or recruited volunteer should document the changes that are made to the process map and have another team member create a few report-out slides that summarize what the event was about, what happened and the go-forward plan. If time doesn't allow you to do this during the event, do it very soon afterwards so that it can be sent out to the team.

Prioritizing initiatives

During the meeting, you will be facilitating the discussion and prioritizing initiatives. Sometimes the prioritization process will be simple. When there is a clear distinction between the value of each initiative and everyone agrees, then you are good to go.

The next step up from discussing and collectively agreeing to the priorities is to give everyone a certain number of votes and allow them to cast their votes on the initiatives they feel are most important. If the initiatives are written out on a white board or on a large easel pad, everyone can come forward and add their allotted tickmarks. If you have them on a spreadsheet and are projecting on the wall, then just go around the room and have everyone cast their vote out loud.

If things get more complex and challenging, you will need to employ a slightly more elaborate group decision making process.

When it comes to group decisions and leadership, some leaders think, "I'm the leader; I make the decisions!" And in some situations, that may be appropriate. But for most things related to teams, it is wise to request input from the group.

I'll never forget the time a new leader said, "Ok, I'm the leader. I'll make the decision." While he had initially asked for feedback from the team, his words sent an unfortunate message:

Your input doesn't matter. I may ask you for it as a gesture of my goodness, but in the end, this is really about me. Leaders who take this approach miss the opportunity to gain the engagement and creative input of the team. Fortunately, there is a better way.

Once a decision point is identified, as a group identify all of the various criteria that will be used to evaluate the options. What matters? List the details and fill in any necessary notes related to why certain criteria are important. Then, based on all the factors, identify a weight for each area, i.e., the percentage of the decision that will be guided by that particular aspect of the thing you are deciding upon. All criteria percentages combined should equal 100 percent.

As an example: If you are buying a home, you may determine location is 25 percent of your decision in addition to all of the other details about the house that make up the remaining 75 percent.

Once you have your weighted criteria, you are ready to evaluate the details of all your options. Pick a rating system: one–five or something similar. Review the information for all of the options. Ask questions. Clarify specifics. Provide the opportunity for team members to present their case and persuade others as to why they would rate something a particular way. Then have each team member "vote" by providing their rating for each of the different aspects that are part of the consideration. Collect the numbers. Review them and ask any outliers to defend their position. If they can't, then take their number out. Average all the votes for each area. Multiply the average rating times the percentage to come up with an overall score for each option.

By going through this, you create an objective decision-making process that engages all team members. Obviously, this last approach requires a little more time. This example may not be the perfect approach for your team. The point is that you need an established procedure for making group decisions before you start the process to save yourself a lot of time and pain.

Post-Meeting Follow-Ups and Follow-Throughs

Make sure you identify the method you will use to keep all participants informed as to progress of the initiatives. A monthly conference call followed with an email summary or an internal blog-post update generally works well.

The takeaway collateral from the event are:
- The improvement plan (with champions, team members, and dates)
- The updated process map (a picture of the map on the wall and the updated electronic version)
- The go-forward schedule
- A few report out slides summarizing the event

Send these out to all participants and other interested parties.

Then your governance team will meet to discuss the follow-ups and follow-throughs. Ideally, the governance team will be getting together every other week or so and at least once per month (depending on the aggressiveness of your timeline and the scope of the improvement initiatives). In addition, you should have a template for champions to use that provides an update which includes a quick summary of the initiative, the team members, what has been done and what remains to be done, as well as any challenges faced by the team.

Make sure the champions are clear who they will be reporting out to, when they will be reporting out, what format to use, who else is on the team (if possible, it is helpful to have each participant in the event be part of a team if not a champion for an initiative) as well as the goal for the initiative and how it connects to the project as a whole. Identify a clear method to measure the success of the initiative and include this in the improvement plan.

CHAPTER 7

7. SUMMARY OF THE SYSTEM

Here's a high-level review of the key elements and benefits of the system for successfully leading teams.

First, internalize the leadership formula ($B=A-C^2$). This formula helps you to bring order to chaos, focus on what is important, mitigate challenges that would hold you back, and move from where you are to where you want to be. This is the essence of leadership and a pattern that you will see over and over in all of the different aspects of this system for leading teams. This is leadership thinking.

When it comes to people, start with respect.

The key to the long-term success of any team is people. When it comes to people, start with respect. As you approach your team and individual team members, whether it is the first time or on a daily basis as problems arise, start with *respect* in mind. It's the right attitude to have if you want to create an environment where people feel respected and are empowered to do their very best work.

Almost as important is to always ask yourself the question, "What do I want to get out of it?" This helps to keep your mind fixed on the longer-term end result that you are looking for rather than just reacting to short-term situations.

> *always ask yourself the question, "What do I want to get out of it?"*

Problems—our natural tendency is to try to avoid them. But the truth is that the flip side of the coin for any problem is that there is a solution waiting to be created. This is a good reminder that there is a hidden value in each problem we face. Teach your team the structure of the A3 problem-solving process so that they become adept at thinking through problems. Capture each problem and put it in front of everyone so the collective minds of the team can work together to solve it.

Learn to listen continually to the voice of your customer so you know what it is that they really want, need, and consider valuable. Your customer needs to define what value is.

Mapping and measuring the work that you do allows you to think about the way value is flowing through your system and where it is not. By learning to see and eliminate waste in your system, more value will flow to your customers which ultimately means more revenue flowing to you.

Structure the collaboration of your team and *share* responsibility for leading. Empower your team members so the team benefits from the structured collaboration, problem solving, and leadership growth as team members share the responsibility for facilitating.

As you engage team members by sharing responsibility for regular meetings, evaluating the performance of the team, and training other team members, team members will grow, get better and feel good about their contribution to the team and their growth.

> *Just as problem-solving is the foundation of improving, the same thought process can lead to innovation.*

Implement a process for regular, collaborative improvement. You have a plan and a structure that brings people together, so you can visualize processes, solve problems collaboratively, and continually develop new ways to improve both the processes and the outcome of the work that you do as a team.

Just as problem-solving is the foundation of improving, the same thought process can lead to innovation. As the lens of your focus shifts from focusing on current products, services and processes to bigger problems in the marketplace, the solutions you develop will begin to look more and more like true innovation.

Here is a quick review of the tools and major events that are part of the system where the leadership thinking, and improvement principles are applied:

The Leadership Formula Arrow
The A3 problem-solving document
Event 1: The daily huddle
Huddle support board
Project support board
Event 2: The weekly game plan team meeting
The 4 Quarters template
Team support board
Event 3: Monthly process improvement events
Process map with pain points and improvement ideas
Process improvement plan

Here is the one-sentence summary for each one:

The Leadership Formula Arrow: Use the arrow to organize your thinking about any leadership situation, whether it be the overall responsibility you have for your team or smaller situations that come up.

The A3 Problem-Solving Document: Use the A3 to outline the details of any problem, including the current state, the root cause(s) of the problem, and the ideal or desired state as well as an initial plan to get there.

The Daily Huddle: Prepare by outlining the major milestones with associated point values for the work you do and then gather the team daily for each team member to discuss 1.) what I did yesterday 2.) the challenges or impediments I am having, and 3.) what I am planning to do today, in order to develop shared responsibility for facilitating, shared accountability to fellow team members and shared problem solving.

The Huddle Support Board: Use this for team members to document their daily points earned, any impediments they are having and any improvement ideas or particular areas of focus for the team.

The Project Support Board: Use this to keep track of all the individual projects that are in process, where they are in the process and how the overall load of projects balances out across the team.

The Weekly Game Plan Meeting: Share the preparation and facilitation of this meeting with team members and review 1.) the team's performance 2.) the plan for improvement 3.) training in an area of importance, and 4.) a celebration and recognition of team member contributions.

The 4 Quarters Template: Use this tool to give team members an easy start to their responsibility to prepare and facilitate part of the weekly meeting.

The Team Support Board: Use this tool to provide a visual overview that anyone can walk by and see of who is on the team, what the team does, how performance is, the plan to improve and any recent rewards or recognition.

The Monthly Process Improvement Event: Gather key stakeholders from the team and outside of the team to analyze the map of the entire process and determine a plan to improve the major pain points within the process.

The Process Map with Pain Points and Improvement Ideas: Use this tool to clarify the process and get all key stakeholders on the same page about the problems within the process and plan to improve them.

The Improvement Plan: Use this tool to clarify the individual improvement initiatives, who owns them and when they are expected to be completed.

Each of these areas should have an associated Single-Point-Lesson document that goes along with it and of course your team log that is used to keep track of the outcomes of each event or gathering of the team.

As you read through these key elements of the system, notice the interplay of vision and problem-solving in the leadership process. Some of the elements are primarily about vision but they require a certain amount of problem solving, whereas others are primarily about problem solving yet they require a certain amount of vision (thinking ahead and creativity). Pretty cool, right?

> *notice the interplay of vision and problem-solving in the leadership process.*

PART 3: TIPS FOR SUCCESS

Chapter 8

8. PITFALLS TO AVOID

The Player Coach Syndrome

Many times, people who have been promoted to "manage" or lead teams were promoted because they were very good players on the team. After becoming a leader, they will try to maintain an individual workload in addition to their managerial responsibilities, so they can proudly say, "Yes, I'm a player/coach." to avoid the false guilt that comes with thinking that leadership by itself doesn't require enough "real work."

> *"The physics just don't work for the player coach model."*

One colleague used to say, "The physics just don't work for the player coach model." That means that you cannot physically be "on the field" playing (doing front-line work) and be on the sidelines coaching (leadership work). You can't be in two places at once. If you are on the field doing front-line work, then you are not doing the leadership work, and when you understand the role of leadership and have a system for effectively leading a team, you recognize that there is real work to do.

There is organizational work, planning work, facilitating work, coaching work, mentoring work, etc. Even delegation properly requires a certain amount of making sure that people are confident in what they are doing. When you really understand the full-time job of leadership, then you won't try to spend time as a player on the field.

Data Phobia

The most important thing regarding data: Don't be afraid of it! Get comfortable with it. Pause for a second, and let that sink in. Decide here and now that you are going to make data your friend. When you are friends with someone, it doesn't mean you always understand everything about them. You don't. And that is why you ask questions to deepen your relationship.

> *Decide here and now that you are going to make data your friend.*

You must do the same with data. Sometimes data can be a little bit like the ghosts in the Bruce Willis movie *The Sixth Sense*; they scare the bajeebers out of you until you take the time to listen and understand them better.

Don't let seemingly complex data fool you. People often start using "techno-speak" (niche specific language that not everyone is familiar with) when talking about data, but data can be very simple if we take time to understand it and keep it simple.

Let's start with the simple example of measuring a child's height: all you do is make a mark on the wall and record the height, and then later, make another mark on the wall and record the new height. With that little bit of information, you can make all types of observations: the child grew four inches; they grew 5 percent; the amount of their growth was greater than the prior year, etc.

Obviously, the work you do will likely be more complex, but if you can simplify it to what matters and keep track of your daily numbers for individuals and the team, then data is not so challenging. You can start to speak very intelligently about the work being done by your team. You just have to determine what is important and measure it. That is what this system does for you.

When we reviewed the Daily Support Board, we talked about keeping track of the daily challenges or impediments that come up. These challenges also become numbers: the number of challenges that have come up and the number that have been solved. When you can add numbers and percentages to something and speak to how it is changing over time, it becomes very powerful information.

Here are a couple of examples: "We solved 80 percent of our daily impediments within forty-eight hours over the last two weeks." "By making this one adjustment to our software, we reduced our trouble tickets by 60 percent over the last month."

One team I used to lead was constantly complaining about the speed of the computers. At first it just sounded like standard grumbling; a lot of times we are not fully satisfied with our work technology.

Eventually, it wasn't just one team member from time to time; it became the entire team complaining at least once a day. Instead of just saying "Our computers are too slow; we want new ones!" we decided to measure it for a week. As each team member sat and watched "the spinning doughnut," they recorded how long they waited and then totaled it up at the end of the day. I knew it was bad, but I had no idea how bad!

When all the numbers were put together, they showed that the team was spending up to 20 percent of their day just waiting for their computer to catch up. Can you guess what happened when we were able to present those numbers and obtain better computers? Productivity jumped!

So, make sure that you are measuring the things that you care about. Lay the data out in a way that you can visualize the trends and understand how things are going so that you can set targets for how you want them to be. Set up your system for measuring, recording past numbers, and reporting. Then test them out and modify your system as needed.

You can always boil data down to something very understandable: How much money did we spend? How much did we make? What was the difference between the two? How does that compare to where we wanted to be or to how we did last year? If we missed our targets, what were the root causes of the reasons and what can we do to counteract them? As long as you keep in mind that data can be simple, and help you improve, data can be fun and extremely valuable.

One of Coach K's favorite questions to ask before looking at any data (or going into any meeting for that matter) was "What do you want to get out of it?" So, when you are looking at data, make sure you ask the same question: What do I want to get out of this? What do I want to know by looking at this data?

"What do you want to get out of it?" - Coach K

By utilizing this system and keeping track of your data, you should have all the information you need to report regularly on the key performance metrics for your team. This should include a measure of productivity, a measure of cycle time or speed of delivery, and some measure of quality which may be based on customer feedback or reporting of errors, etc.

Thinking You Must Know It All

There is a dangerous temptation to believe that you must know it all or be the most knowledgeable to be a good leader. While it can be helpful to have insights and background to understand the context of certain business environments, to lead well, other things are just as if not more important. Look at the results of a survey conducted by Google about what makes a good manager:

A large internal study of successful managers called Project Oxygen, started in 2009, outlined the key characteristics of good managers and provided the playbook for successful team leadership within the company. Look at the top three characteristics:

- They're good coaches.
- They empower their team and don't micro-manage.
- They express interest in their team members' success and personal well-being.

At first, these results might seem like typical, common, everyday results. But look at the item that was last in importance on Google's list:

- They have key technical skills that help them advise the team.

For some companies, this finding may be less impactful. But it is impressive for a data and technology company to recognize that technical skills come behind coaching and empowerment skills for team leaders. The seemingly small shift from focusing on technical strengths to focusing on the person's ability to coach and bring out the best in people is an important message to new leaders: leadership is about people more than technical expertise.

Give it Time to Grow

It takes time to mature this system. You are not going to be perfect on day one. As you implement different aspects of the system, you will need to evaluate how effective that piece is and modify it to improve your overall process.

Seeing team members grow, develop, and be empowered and engaged in their work is extremely satisfying. Instead of trying to motivate them in some arbitrary way, you will notice that team members are self-motivated and successful as they grow in their leadership skills.

> *Seeing team members grow, develop, and be empowered and engaged in their work is extremely satisfying.*

Just as kids and trees take time to grow, you will need to give this system time to mature with your team. You should also see some immediate and profound results but be patient, knowing that you are moving in the right direction.

Take it step by step. Start by incorporating the Leadership Formula and principles into your thinking. Then teach the A3 problem-solving method and get used to using it as problems come up. Prepare and implement the huddle. After you have been doing the huddle for a couple of months and you feel that your team is confident with it, add the weekly game plan.

It is possible to jump right into a process improvement event but having the other elements in place first will help to sustain the momentum and effectively implement the initiatives identified.

CHAPTER 9

9. LEADERSHIP QUALITIES

Know Thyself

Knowing yourself means getting comfortable in your own skin. You do this by not trying to be someone else and gaining a better understanding of who you really are.

Let's say you have a friend you admire who is funny and engaging with others. But your personality is more contemplative. You think it would be great to be more like your friend, so you try it out. But it just doesn't work. It doesn't fit or feel comfortable. Why? You are trying to wear someone else's skin. Wear your own. Figure out who you are and then be yourself 110 percent.

You can start leading without knowing yourself, but eventually not knowing who you are and who you want to be will negatively impact you and your team.

What does "knowing thyself" really include? For starters, you should be self-aware enough to know whether you are an introvert or an extrovert (or what mix of the two). It is important to know what types of activities give you energy and those that drain you.

Then I would recommend taking a personality assessment such as DISC or StrengthsFinder. These are helpful to better understand your natural personality tendencies and the type of work, activities, and people interaction that are likely to be more fulfilling. No matter the bent of your personality, you can lead. Understanding yourself will help you to lead better.

More importantly, it really helps you to better understand and relate with others, which is essential when you are leading a team. When you don't really understand who you are and how you operate, you may tend to slip into the mindset that other people should be just like you.

When we find out people are not just like us or we have friction because we are different, we assume that there is something wrong with the other person. If they were only more like us, things would be fine, we think. Start with knowing yourself so you can better understand others and lead better.

The confidence that comes from being comfortable in your own skin is essential for good leadership. Some refer to this as a positive self-image and this is sort of true. But many leaders have such a positive self-image of themselves but don't really know who they are, and they become un-relatable; they aren't real. They can't be authentic because it is clear they are overcompensating for some shortcomings that they don't want others to know about. Because they are covering something up, they are unable to practice the natural humility that comes with being comfortable with yourself.

The flip side of this problem is just as bad. If we are so humble that we degrade ourselves or place ourselves lower than we are, all in the lofty name of humility, we do just as much injustice as someone with an overinflated ego. We have to find the middle ground where we recognize our own strengths but don't try to take all the credit for them, and we recognize our weaknesses but don't worry so much about them. When we do that, we become fully relatable and able to lead others better.

Once you "know thyself," you can begin to really appreciate others for who they are. You will be a better leader for it.

Own Your Attitude

I'll never forget the day I realized that I was the owner of my own attitude. I literally jumped out of bed. The day before I'd been reading *The Magic of Thinking Big* by David J. Schwartz, PH.D., and when my eyes opened, the power of this truth hit me. A good amount of our circumstances may be beyond our control, but we have the power to adjust the way we interpret them and what we do about it.

Just coming to the full realization that you are in control of your attitude can be monumental. Many people allow their attitude to be determined by how others treat them, what the weather is like, or how they perceive they are doing at whatever they are trying to accomplish. All of these things are subjective and if you allow things to determine your attitude, it will go up or down depending on which way the wind is blowing.

"Don't be the thermometer, be the thermostat."

- John Maxwell

Once you come to the conclusion that you are the ultimate judge and jury who determines your attitude, you have a leg up and a key component that is critical for winning the long game. As leadership expert John Maxwell says, "Don't be the thermometer, be the thermostat" (*The Winning Attitude*). Set the temperature, set the mood. . . . Don't be subject to the moods of others or the external circumstances."

Humor and Happiness

Shortly after our company was acquired by our top competitor, we were all gathered together in one large hotel ballroom. Emotions were high. Curiosity peeked. Political antennas were sky high as everyone prepared to jockey for position. As the CEO took the stage, you could feel the excitement and the tension of the atmosphere.

Without much ado, he went into a joke, which at first seemed like a true story. He incorporated leaders from both companies, and the initial parts of the story were something that could have happened. A party that took place where everyone dressed up as an emotion. And then he did it... the joke became one of those offend-everyone, inappropriate jokes...and everyone roared! In a weird way, it was perfect. Not because I am a big fan of inappropriate jokes, but because he was able to use humor to diffuse a tense situation and bring people together.

I looked across to our old HR team wondering how they would respond. In our old company, people had been fired for less. Would they laugh too?

If anyone wondered before who was in charge, they now knew. He was. And everything was going to be just fine. The joke cut through the ice and gave everyone permission to just relax.

Humor, on occasion, can work such miracles. I am not recommending you tell your team inappropriate jokes on a daily basis. But incorporating humor into your team dynamics shows that you are human. It shows that in addition to knowing how to work smart and work hard, you also know how to have fun and enjoy being around the people on your team.

"Sorry, I'm good on happy."

If I picked up this book at a bookstore and browsed the table of contents, I suppose I would turn directly to this section on humor and happiness. Because, think about it, who doesn't want more of both of those? Who would say "Sorry, I'm good on happy; let's do something else for a while"? No one. Everybody wants more of both of those things. And your team members do too.

This does not mean that your job as a leader is to keep everybody happy or in stitches, but it does mean you need to be aware that these things are important to people and, therefore, to your team. Your team will work better together if these ingredients are included in the mix of interactions and collaborations.

Do a quick Google search on "humor in leadership," and you will see results like:

➢ "Study finds humor gives leaders the edge"

➢ "Eight ways humor will make you a better leader"

➢ "Three big reasons humor benefits your leadership"

Read any of the various articles and you will find the many positive aspects of humor in leadership. Whether or not you are disarming hostile situations, connecting with people, or freeing your mind to creatively solve problems, humor has many benefits.

Burnout happens when you become overwhelmed by the environment around you and all the things flying around your head; the problems you are trying to solve, the situations you are trying to deal with.

How can you avoid this? Connect with others through humor. Let's break this last sentence down a little bit. First, **connect**: you have to remain part of a group; don't go off alone. Next, **others**: you have to have other people involved to bounce ideas off, to share concerns, to brainstorm solutions, to help get things done. This keeps you from owning and internalizing problems that don't truly belong to you; they are just part of a situation and you are there to help remedy them, not to let them bring you down. And last but not least, **humor**. Adding humor to any situation makes it more enjoyable and frees up the creative side of your brain to come up with more creative solutions.

Sharing humor is a great connector. You know there are things that you find funny so share those. Listen for the things that your team finds funny.

Frequently leaders remain distant to avoid the messiness that sometimes comes with getting close to people. When you have an organized system for collaboration, problem solving, and accountability, you can afford to connect. In fact, you need to. Connecting with others and inviting humor into the workplace makes for a happy environment.

Let's be clear: work is not supposed to always be full of happiness, unicorns, and rainbows. It can be hard and sometimes gets messy. People have personal issues that will get in the way of work. Sometimes they will not get along well with teammates. Feelings will get hurt. Offenses will happen. Customers may leave. It happens. It's life. Life with people is messy.

One of my favorite sayings is "Where there are no oxen, the manger is clean but abundant crops come by the strength of the ox." (Proverbs 14:4 ESV). Are people oxen? No. But they are messy! On the other hand, if you want everything to be clean and tidy, you won't get much done. There will be obstacles to overcome and you will need help from other people.

Health, happiness, joy, kindness, creativity, and overcoming obstacles—these things go together. When your mind is not bogged down with concerns, it is free to be creative and solve problems. This does not mean that you only ever see the good in every situation, the silver lining with no cloud. It means that when you look at the "bad" stuff, you are able to see beyond it. How? Because you don't view it as the end result.

It may be the current state of things, but it isn't final and so your mind doesn't get stuck on it, feel upset, feel concerned, or anything else that will essentially stop your brain from working on the problem and working toward your ultimate desired outcome.

In addition to being open to a little levity in the workplace, remember to keep asking yourself the question, "What do you want to get out of it?" Especially during difficult situations.

Not happy with someone's driving and considering cutting them off? What do you want to get out of it? Have a disagreement with a family member and decide to confront them to prove that you are in the right? What do you want to get out of it? Going into an important meeting? What do you want to get out of it? Life? What do you want to get out of it?

Asking yourself this simple question helps keep your mind on the end result you are looking for—which in turn, helps guide the actions that you take now, which will be (after asking yourself this question) more lined up with your long-term goals.

Love and Leadership

"I may not be a smart man, but I know what love is."
- Forrest Gump.

Forrest Gump had it figured out! So did Phil Jackson. Michael Jordan, who many consider to be one of the greatest basketball players of all time, has six NBA championship rings. Phil Jackson, as both a player and coach, has eleven. In his book *Eleven Rings,* he breaks down leadership quickly to include one very core component based on what he has seen to be necessary for teams to accomplish the impossible and win championships: Love.

Why? Because love means caring for others and self-sacrifice. It also means seeing the desired end result beyond tough situations or the way people are currently acting. It means not giving up on people just because they are not exactly as we would like them to be.

Another key attribute of a loving leader is one who forgives. Don't let people problems fester. Bring people together in private to address them face-to-face and help them understand how important it is for the team to get over their differences. When I was an ankle-biter, our daycare teachers used to make anyone having difficulties sit on the bench together until we resolved our differences enough to shake hands. Sometimes, even as adults, we need to sit on the bench until we can shake hands.

Here are some of the characteristics I would look for, in addition to love, in a good leader:

- Competent
- Clear vision
- Collaborative
- Organized
- Knows how to organize people
- Understands people
- Selects good people to be around
- Good teacher
- Familiar with the environment of competition
- Persuasive
- Good negotiator
- Kind
- Generous
- Humble
- Confident

Evaluate these for yourself. Maybe you don't agree with some. That is ok. Make your own list to better understand what is most important to you and then check to see how much the lists match up.

Chapter 10

10. REMEMBER THIS

Rule #1

The 60 percent rule = 60 percent is good enough to get started. Perfection is not required in the beginning. Just as the idea from Woody Allan to "just show up" can get us started, the 60 percent rule allows us to keep going rather than bogging ourselves down with the details of trying to get something 100 percent right, right out of the gate.

In most cases, continuing to move forward is more important than being perfect. The old saying "You can't steer a parked car" is true! Keep moving forward! Then it is much easier to perfect things as you go. Striving for perfection is good. Only accepting perfection to the point where it immobilizes you is bad. Don't let it happen to your team. Keep moving. . . then steer.

Rule #2

Train the leaders around you rather than trying to do it all yourself. Hint: you can't do it all by yourself!

One of the most missed areas of focus for new leaders, especially when others are busy with other things and don't stay engaged on their own, is to forget to keep other leaders informed, updated, and involved in the process. If you don't do this, it will cost you down the line. Gain support from other leaders and keep them informed, updated, and involved.

When you think you are at the finish line of a project and excited about the results, your leader may engage and throw things off course—usually right at the last minute. Why? Because they need to be informed. Even if they continue to remain disengaged, if you've done your part to keep them informed and a situation arises, you will be able to overcome objections, only because you have kept them in the loop during the decision making and doing of the process.

Hint: you can't do it all by yourself!

Rule #3

Keep your thoughts on the end result that you are looking for rather than other people's bad behavior. When you focus on what people are doing wrong, anger clouds your judgement and you may act inappropriately—making the situation worse. If you stay fixed on what you really want to get out of the situation, you are less likely to blow up, and you will be in a position to have a productive conversation with no hurt feelings or injured relationships. It all comes back to asking the key question: What do you want to get out of it?

Chapter 11

11. LOOKING FORWARD

Leading in the Technology Age

Some of us grew up watching two favorite Saturday morning cartoons: *The Flintstones* and *The Jetsons*. As you may know, one of these cartoons is about a family in the Stone Age and the other is about a family in the future.

Keep in mind that at the time, there were approximately three and a half channels you could watch on television. The good thing was that you didn't have to spend an hour scrolling through all of the options on Netflix before figuring out what to watch; you were simply happy if anything was on, and especially if it was one of your favorite cartoons or maybe *The Dukes of Hazard* or *The Six Million Dollar Man* (why was he always battling Bigfoot...?).

Even now, as I look back, those days seem like the stone ages of television. But what about the future?

How much of what was presented as futuristic in *The Jetsons* has already come to pass? Robot maids, flying cars, and video chat (without the façade hair for Jane)? Our dog is certainly just as loved and almost as troublesome as Astro.

Think about the future. Imagine being there already and looking back on this time period. What will this age, our current time, eventually be known for and referred to? The computer age? The internet age? The digital age? The social media age? The artificial intelligence age? The age of disruption?

No matter the state of technological development, the need for good leadership has always been and will always be present. But technology and its impact on society does have an impact on what is possible in terms of communication and what works best in terms of leadership.

The state of technical and economic development in the Industrial Age and the early Post-Industrial Age (as a shift began from manufacturing toward more knowledge and creative work) allowed for autocratic, command and control, top-down only style of leadership. Maybe that form of leadership was the most efficient for the needs of the time. Today is different. The environment we live in has changed dramatically.

Social media has certainly had an impact on our political environment. It has also changed the way businesses communicate and connect with customers. Platforms like Google, Amazon, Facebook, YouTube, Shopify, Slack, and video conferencing tools (in addition to email in general) have changed where and how people can do work and their marketing access to consumers.

Compare buying a Facebook ad for ten dollars a day to what it cost for a company or product to advertise on television twelve years ago. The "democratization" of business via the internet has spread the power to earn money to the masses, changing the dynamic between employers and employees. Whereas employees in the past may have just been happy to have the opportunity to receive a paycheck, we now want to also have work/life balance and be fulfilled in other ways. This changes the way leaders must lead.

As a society, we are fairly proud of ourselves right about now in terms of technological development. The big question is, can we keep the rest of it together long enough to see how technology will continue to develop? Technology builds on itself. Each advancement building on what is known and what has already been done. Sometimes slowly and incrementally and sometimes in big leaps.

Those that can see ahead have already recognized a conundrum we have created for ourselves: artificial intelligence and robotics will eliminate the need for people to do many jobs they have done in the past so what will all of those people do who used to perform those jobs now done by machines?

While we don't know exactly what needs or work will be created by technological advancement (look at all the people who do coding and software development now—a job that didn't exist in the past), one thing is clear: many people will be doing something different than they do today.

People will do what they can do that machines cannot. And that answer is simple: create. People, by nature, are creative. But for people to be creative requires a style and approach to leadership that allow creativity and yet still stays organized and accomplishes goals.

And of course, they will be working together with other people to do so. This means people must figure out how to better work together in teams in order to maximize their capabilities and be creative and productive in ways that create value and, therefore, earn compensation.

In today's world of constant change and technological development, there is a convergence of the need for leadership and management skills. There is no longer a constant state to be managed, or points of change requiring leadership, but rather a constant state of change requiring collaborative leadership and a management style that can solve problems quickly, adapt to change, and innovate on demand.

Many people accept that "command and control" style leadership is not the most desirable form of leadership. At times that form of leadership is effective to some degree or even necessary—possibly in combat situations where ground troops have no insights into local conditions or where the leader is so inspired or intelligent that their genius merits a sort of "bowing down" no matter what their other inconsistencies or personality quirks might be. Other times, it may be used when nothing else seems to be working.

So, if "command and control" is not the way to go, then what form of leadership is best? What form of leadership would enable an organization to perform at its highest potential? For a business operating in today's modern economy, where mechanization, computers and artificial intelligence are in the process of replacing many tasks and, ultimately, the jobs performed in the past by humans, this is an extremely important and timely question. Without a solid answer, organizations and teams of people are left to the managerial whims and mixed flavors of leadership randomly compiled and in various stages of development.

Clearly there must be a more dynamic relationship and exchange of ideas between leaders and team members within the organization in order for a business to become everything it is capable of becoming—ultimately to fulfill its full purpose and reason for being. In such a situation, maximized individual performance plus maximized group performance plus great leadership would equal excellence, greatness, and purpose.

In the past, to achieve similar types of results, the company would place the bulk of the weight on the characteristics or qualities of the leader. And of course, the character of any leader will always be important. However, the system of organization and interactions of a group is the key to creating organizations that perform at their highest potential. The system of leadership and organization is just as important as the person in leadership.

Many corporate leaders are willing to chant the mantra "Employees are our greatest asset!" only to cut headcount as the first reaction to financial challenges. The hard truth is that employees that are only used in machine-like performance of tasks—following instructions that can be done just as well or better by technology—are indeed a liability to a company.

However, when employees are empowered to become high-powered problem solvers, efficient implementers, and creative innovators, they then become a company's greatest asset. This is only possible with the right mindset and a system for leading people that recognizes this reality and empowers people to contribute at their full potential.

Should we simply resign ourselves to technology-enabled job destruction and establish some form of "minimum living wage" so people can continue to survive without necessarily doing work or adding value? Or is there a way to organize and lead people in such a way that their talents and abilities are an essential ingredient (a "most valuable asset") to the full performance of the organization—similar to the way sports teams win when each player is at their best and the team is working together at its best with a great coach?

Remote Work and Social Media

Depending on which report you read, remote work is either trending up or back down from a new high. Either way, you will likely work with team members from different locations. You may as well build it into your plans.

Even in companies that have no formal policy for remote workers, it is likely that the company has multiple offices and staff who are in the field and need to communicate and collaborate. Whether your company has a formal remote worker strategy or not, the use of collaboration tools and structured collaboration is likely.

There are some simple steps you can take to ensure that you keep remote team members engaged. The first thing to do is to establish the regular cadence of the daily huddle, the weekly game plan meeting and monthly improvement events. Then, you can add in a dial-in number for daily huddles, a login for the weekly meeting, and if possible, I would recommend having remote team members travel in for an improvement event at least once a year if not more.

The increase in remote workers has been accompanied by the advent of collaboration chat apps and other social media tools. This is great news because it is easier to keep in touch.

This includes team messaging tools like Slack, Facebook groups, video conference tools like Zoom, project management tools, cloud file management tools, and others such as workflow, design, or software development collaboration tools. But no matter how good technology gets, there is still a benefit to organized and structured collaboration.

Don't try to replace organization, structure, and strategy with tools alone. It won't work. These tools are a little bit like a super power: if the team members don't know how to use them, they won't do them a lot of good.

You may end up with some random communication, and in some cases, it may even fix a problem or help to deal with a situation. But if you want to have a high-powered and highly empowered team, you need to give them more than just tools. They need to have a structure and a strategy that makes it clear when to incorporate their super powers.

Important Note about the System

Many of the concepts covered here are not new. Most of the system described in the following pages comes from a "Lean" based approached that Coach K taught me while we worked together. He, in turn, learned it while at Ford and received training directly from experts at Toyota.

Of course, Coach K made some of his own modifications and I have as well. As most Lean experts will tell you, Lean concepts and principles are applied by customizing them to the local environment. Because of this, the processes themselves are constantly improving. Most of the underlying principles of course, remain the same.

I believe these principles and the processes and procedures they help to create are more relevant today than ever. Why? Because of the world we live in - globalized economy where automation and artificial intelligence are on the rise. We must learn to maximize our effectiveness as small groups and teams if we are going to succeed.

Learning to lead teams is not only the foundation for companies but also for sports teams, for families, and for many other types of groups. The principles and concepts outlined here apply to many different areas. Of course, they may need some customization in practice to fit different environments, but the principles apply, and they work.

The Call to Leadership

The rewards of leading a team can be tremendous. Yes, it can be stressful. It involves people, and therefore it can be messy. People are messy—but they are also amazing, and they can give you something that you won't get anywhere else—the satisfaction of knowing that you have worked together and that you are both the better for it—you've created something that is bigger than the sum of the parts.

When done right, people working together can have a multiplier effect. And, it is very true that you, as a leader, will make a big difference in the lives of others. Not just because you helped them to be a better person, but because you helped them to develop talents and skills they didn't even know they had—or were sure they didn't have! It is similar in a way to the same power and influence that teachers sometimes have which can have a profound impact on students' lives.

Maybe you have heard the call to leadership but hesitated. You felt like you were being asked to step out of the comfortable boat you were in and walk on the water. Or you've accepted the call but have struggled to do it as well as you would like. Maybe you are even doing well but recognize that more is possible, and you want what is best. I've been there, and I know that this system can help you to get to where you want to be.

The truth is we are all called to leadership. To lead ourselves first and then who knows—A start-up? A team? A business unit? A large company? Some other type of organization? With the right principles, processes, and personal development, it is possible to not only do it but to do it well. Enjoy the journey...

Free Downloads

Go to: TheLeadershipFormulaBook.com for FREE templates and to subscribe to our newsletter.

Acknowledgements

Have you heard the story of how bees produce honey? A single bee cannot produce honey alone. It is always a group effort. One bee gathers the nectar from the flower blossom and stores it in its "honey-tummy". Later it spits it out and another bee eats it, followed by another bee and another bee, each adding its own contribution until ultimately all the nectar is spit out into honeycomb, and voila! You've got honey—a work of art created by many.

In the same way, this book required the contributions of multiple leaders and thinkers, whose ideas and concepts have been mulled over, employed, modified, and ultimately included in this book.

I would like to recognize some of the coaches and leaders from my life who taught me important lessons and helped me to move forward on my leadership journey. . . my dad, my mom, Tom Ryan (Little League coach), Larry Johnson (frame shop owner), Doyle Borts (gas station owner), Stan Malless (college English professor), Paul Zastro (prior Editor of The Simpsonian), Noah Lacona (Noah's Ark Restaurante founder), Jim Webb (my first boss in Texas), Hank Ffrench (my boss from "da Bronx"), Tim Galpin (impactful leadership professor at the University of Dallas), Ron Geguzys (Lean Six Sigma coach and mentor), Charles Hagood (healthcare thought leader, entrepreneur and author), Maureen Gender (a classy, natural leader), Dan James (able to simplify any complex situation with a good analogy), Ken Thomson (the all-around leader), Nick Khawaja (Lean sensei extraordinaire), Jason Erdell (healthcare thought leader), Scott Gressett (healthcare leader and my last boss), John Bardis (one of the best CEOs I have had the pleasure of working with), Jason Adams (advisor and founder DayOne Consulting), Matt Brown (entrepreneur and advisor), Brice McBeth (digital marketing agency owner and author), Debbie Sardone (founder, speaker and author), Chandler Bolt (SPS founder and bestselling author), Scott Allan (bestselling author and coach), Wesley Wiley (executive coach) and many more.

Bibliography

Forest Gump. Dir. Robert Zemeckis. Perf. Tom Hanks. Paramount Pictures, 1994. Film

The Jerk. Dir. Carl Reiner. Perf. Steve Martin. Universal Studios, 1979. Film

Kung Fu Panda. Dir. Mark Osborne and John Stevenson. Perf. (voice) Dustin Hoffman. DreamWorks Animation, 2008. Film

Star Wars: The Last Jedi. Dir. Rian Johnson. Perf. Daisy Ridley. Disney, 2017. Film

Schwartz, David Joseph. *The Magic of Thinking Big*. New York: Simon and Schuster, 1959. Print

Maxwell, John. *The Winning Attitude*. Nashville: Thomas Nelson, Inc., 1993. Print

Jackson, Phil. *Eleven Rings*. New York: Penguin Books, 2013. Print

McNally, Jess. "Earth's Most Stunning Natural Fractal Patterns." *Wired.com*, Sept. 10, 2010, www.wired.com/2010/09/fractal-patterns-in-nature/

The Holy Bible, ESV Study Bible. Wheaton: Crossway, 2011. Print

ABOUT THE AUTHOR

Justin grew up wandering around Iowa and spent time studying in Grenoble, France where the mountains are a little taller and the skiing is pretty good. He taught and coached middle school in Des Moines, worked in the investment business in Chicago and then spent over twelve years in healthcare in the Dallas area. He earned an MBA from the University of Dallas and a Lean Six Sigma Black Belt from Air Academy Associates in Colorado Springs. He and his wife reside in Flower Mound, Texas with their two kids, Samuel and Hannah and their dog, Maggie.

Made in the USA
Lexington, KY
28 December 2018